GOTTA LOVE
THIS COUNTRY!

GOTTA LOVE THIS COUNTRY!

PETER FITZSIMONS

ALLEN&UNWIN
SYDNEY·MELBOURNE·AUCKLAND·LONDON

First published in 2015

Copyright © Peter FitzSimons 2015

Cartoons copyright © Reg Lynch 2015

Allen & Unwin
83 Alexander Street
Crows Nest NSW 2065
Australia
Phone: (61 2) 8425 0100
Email: info@allenandunwin.com
Web: www.allenandunwin.com

Cataloguing-in-Publication details are available
from the National Library of Australia
www.trove.nla.gov.au

ISBN 978 1 76029 048 1

Set in 12/17 pt Minion Pro by Midland Typesetters, Australia
Printed and bound in Australia by Griffin Press

10 9 8 7 6 5 4 3 2

Other works by Peter FitzSimons

Basking in Beirut and Other Adventures with Peter FitzSimons
Nick Farr Jones
Rugby Stories
Hitch-hiking for Ugly People
The Rugby War
Everyone but Phar Lap
Everyone and Phar Lap
FitzSimons on Rugby
Beazley
Nancy Wake
John Eales
Nene
Kokoda
The Story of Skilled and Frank Hargrave
Steve Waugh
Great Australian Sports Champions
Little Theories of Life
The Ballad of Les Darcy
Tobruk
Kokoda
And Now for Some Light Relief
Charles Kingsford Smith and Those Magnificent Men
A Simpler Time
Mawson
Batavia
Eureka
Ned Kelly
Carlo Salteri and the Story of Transfield
Gallipoli
Fromelles and Pozières

INTRODUCTION

It was a Friday, nudging on twenty years ago. There I was, about to head out to lunch, when my *Sydney Morning Herald* sports editor Steve Meacham called across the editorial floor, 'Paul's not in today, can you do "*Inside Running*"?'

Bugger.

'Inside Running' was the light wrap-up of the week's sporting events, which I had no particular interest in. But . . .

'Yes, Boss.'

I smashed it out in about 45 minutes flat – once over lightly – throwing together the news of the week, the best quotes, a couple of sporting vignettes, a bit of a rant on something or other, and I'll tell you who was my uncle. Bob was my uncle!

And I made it to the lunch.

Come the Monday, back at the office, a strange thing was happening. There was a huge reaction—phone calls, letters, *compliments* from colleagues . . . and from the Editor-in-Chief.

Why not do it again this week? Yes, boss.

This time I actually put some time into it, and some effort, and the reaction was even stronger. Somehow this kind of itsy-bitsy journalism, constantly changing angles and subjects, suited my short attention-span and that of many readers. I soon took over the whole thing every week and Steve renamed it 'The Fitz Files'. In no time at all, I loved it and it became my focus, gathering yarns throughout the week. But now here's a funny thing . . .

Always, the thing that got the biggest reaction was not my newsy bit, nor my rants, nor my bits of philosophical sporting whimsy. No, what people most loved, it seemed, was the heart-warming stuff, the stuff far away from sports' elite level, and back to the grass roots . . . sport, the way sport was always meant to be.

I started out using a 'Gawd, I love this city'–riff to introduce each section, which soon morphed into 'Gotta love this city', and then, 'Gotta love this country!'

The broad idea was to celebrate all the great things about sport—at all levels—to note with wonder how lucky we all are to be able to enjoy them, with all their quirks, colour and romance.

What you hold in your hands, is the first tranche of the best of these stories. I do hope you enjoy the reading, as I have enjoyed the writing.

Peter FitzSimons

Who was that beanied balladeer?

The scene is a packed railway carriage pulling out of the station after the Springboks have been put to the sword. At one end of the carriage stands a huge South African man in a Bok jersey and beanie, with a slightly crestfallen look and carrying, of all things, a huge piano accordion. Opposite him stand two slightly drunken Australian supporters in Wallaby jerseys.

They look at him. He looks at them.

One of the Australians then speaks: 'Come on, Mr Piano Accordion Man, how about a tune?'

The South African immediately brightens. He begins to play and sing. Fantastically! 'The lion sleeps tonight'.

In short order, the entire carriage is singing, clapping and stomping along to song after song as Strathfield, Summer Hill and Petersham stations fall back in the night to the sounds of 'She'll Be Coming Round The Mountain', 'If I Was a Rich Man', 'House of the Rising Sun' etc. As an interlude, the bloke sings an opera aria in rich baritone and also a South African folk tune to which all his countrymen in the carriage sing along, while the Australians simply laugh and clap along to the beat.

When he makes to sit down nearing Newtown station, the entire carriage roars for more, and he obliges as they proceed, rockin'-rollin'-ridin' all the way to Central.

People leave the carriage, still singing, each one warmly thanking the bloke for his efforts. He glows appreciatively in return, and disappears into the night. Gotta love this country!

Hell & leather

As part of the Host City Marathon, I was in the last gaggle of the 5,500 runners struggling up Oxford Street just after 7am, huffing and puffing and sweating up a storm when a large group of leather-whips-and-chains boys were emerging from an obviously TORRID all-night session at one of the clubs just up from Whitlam Square.

Both groups regarded each other a little warily, and then the leather men started clapping us and cheering very good-heartedly only to receive equally warm cheers from the runners. Fellow sufferers all, there was instant empathy between us.

At that moment, whhhhhheeeeeeeee! the first of the wheel-chair racers came zooming down the other side of the road, with the rising morning sun on their backs and the whistling wind in their hair, to be cheered by the whole damn lot of us.

Let us pray . . .

Billy Freeman was attending the Bulldogs–Souths game at the Sydney Showground and standing in a queue to get food at half-time when he saw what he describes as 'the strangest sight I have ever seen at a football game'.

'A Muslim man, aged about 20–21, wearing a Canterbury jersey and a reversed baseball cap, was kneeling on his prayer mat facing Mecca and worshipping Allah on the concourse of the eastern grandstand. With the hysteria surrounding people of the Muslim culture created by politicians lately, I was worried he may be abused or something.

'But to their credit, people, albeit a bit bemused, left him alone. I am told he made it back in time for the second-half kick-off!'

Golden oldies bowled over on flight of fancy

Just a few weeks ago the old and the bold from the Hunters Hill Cats Golden Oldies Rugby team were on a flight bound for some rugby revelry on the Gold Coast, and one of my spies was there. The fact that the airline had not spotted them as a rugby team was likely due to the fact that they had booked as lady bowlers, and therefore were all seated together. Mistake. Big mistake. The flight attendants on that day were headed by the truly gorgeous Brenda and . . .

And as the drinks trolley did its job, and the golden oldies focused progressively more on her lovely form, they soon forgot their baldness, creaking joints and obesity and were taken back to their youth, back as far as 1977 when they had gone through the entire season undefeated. The more they gazed at Brenda, the more they remembered, until, somewhere about 9,000 metres over Tweed Heads, it happened . . .

From the midst of this drooling mob came: 'Hey, Brenda, what's ya muvva's phone number?'

Mall rats

Roy Dunlop was at Castle Hill shopping mall last week* when he took a well-earned rest. *Dum de dum dum dum.* Watching the passing parade. Then suddenly he realised he was sitting opposite a family of five: mum, dad, two teenage boys and a teenage girl.

'An obvious domestic was in progress and I was riveted to my seat with that cool and oppressive feeling one gets on such an occasion. Just as I was starting to make my exit, mother turned to teenage daughter and said: "Are you really telling me that you are supporting Germany in the finals on Sunday?!?"'

*6 July 2002, one week after the 2002 FIFA World Cup had concluded

Serenaded

I have been reliably informed that two weeks ago when Carlton took on the Fremantle Dockers in an AFL match, John Elliott, the former Elders IXL, Carlton and Liberal Party boss, turned up with a notably gorgeous young woman.

(Cue Raymond Chandler: *'She was a blonde. A blonde for a bishop to kick a hole in a stained-glass window for.'*)

What did the Freo crowd do? All together, they stood and warmed to chorus of Joe Jackson's song 'Is she really going out with him?'

Olympic rings

A couple of weeks ago, I gratuitously asked whether, besides Princess Mary and Prince Whatsit, and Roger Federer and his new wife Mirka, did any other happy couple first meet at the Sydney Olympics and ... And how funny I should say that, because I am told that early in 2000 a bloke by the name of Richard, just back from two years' backpacking, scored a job in the media centre, imagining that he would have unrestricted access to each and every athletic event, interspersed with free beer and love—and perhaps a little work—only to find 20-hour days sweating it out in the production room. The only thing that made it tolerable was an attractive brunette journalist by the name of Michelle, who would pop in to say hello.

Just 12 months later they married, and baby no. 4 is due in a few months. At their wedding was Richard's mate, Lucas, who had also met a charmer by the name of Peta while attending an event at the Olympics, and they were soon married too, and also have four kids, a mortgage and have just acquired a mini-van. One Olympics, eight kids, two mini-vans.

First try to Martha

On the banks of St Joseph's College main oval last Sunday afternoon, a day after the Riverview first XV had defeated Joeys before about fifteen thousand people, the Joeys class of 1983 found themselves gathering for a barbecue to celebrate the end of their twenty-year reunion weekend. The steaks went down a treat, as did the wine and beer and, as the sun shone strong, the years fell away.

So, what the hell? Why not play a bit of a muck-around game of footy on the main oval as they did in days of yore? So they did. The only slightly odd thing was the attractive woman who scored the first try.

She was not a wife or a girlfriend but rather a former classmate who, after a brief period of not knowing whether she was Arthur or Martha, had decided on 'Martha' and soon after school finished had the gender altering operation.

Of course it goes without saying that Martha was a winger when at school, but she was warmly welcomed back the night before by the hundred former classmates who attended the reunion, with not one stray bit of bigoted nastiness. It was admirable, as were the thousand or so Joeys boys who stood and applauded Riverview on the previous day after their deserved GPS victory.

Thomas the trier bowls 'em over

You will remember when you and I were young, how our dearest dream was to wear the baggy green. You will sense, as I do, that that desire is not as universal as it was. Still, I like the story of Thomas Mulherin, a nine-year-old who plays in the Pitt Town under-11s in the Hawkesbury Cricket competition.

Throughout this, his first season of playing, he has practised every afternoon with his older brother and mother out in the backyard. A fortnight ago, the mighty Pitt Town made the finals series and the entire family ventured out for the game. Though disappointed to be selected as 13th man, he still stayed at the ground for the entire day with his mum, cheering his team on to victory.

Tom kept practising all the following week, and never breathed a word about the disappointment of not playing. Last Sunday was the final. This time . . . 12th man! Though he still can't get a bat, he can still get to bowl and field under the competition rules, which is really something!

With the whole family watching and willing him on, young Tom, the youngest and near-smallest on the team, finally gets his chance as the skipper throws him the ball. Tom runs in, the ball leaves his hand well, shimmies, dives, bites the pitch and bursts forth . . . A swish, a snick, a dive, an appeal . . .

Goodes' style

Doug Sharp writes:

'The Brownlow Medal is when AFL footballers take a back seat to their wives/girlfriends, and lots of cleavage makes for voyeur TV. But who did our own Swannie medallist Adam Goodes take as his date?? His MUM. Gotta love this country!!!'

Wigs off

On Saturday night at the Sydney Football Stadium before the kick-off of the Waratahs v Brumbies match, the crowd was observing a minute's silence for rugby great Myer Rosenblum when Tim Mornane noticed the Des Tuiavii* fan club at the cricket-ground end of the ground. All the members of the small brigade of devotees had taken their wigs off in respect. But then he noticed one of the band nudge his mate next to him, urging him to remove his wig, he dutifully responded with requisite speed, almost cowering his head with embarrassment that he had not done so sooner.

*A wild-haired Waratah flanker

The wheel deal

Gotta love the people in the Australian bush. Last Saturday more than 200 cyclists tested their mettle over varying distances, leaving from Grafton, Mt Mitchell or Glen Innes and riding to Inverell. One rider, Alex Murray, used the Grafton-to-Inverell ride—228 kilometres—as a training ride for a forthcoming long haul of more than 430 kilometres from Inverell to Brisbane, to raise money for 'Team Adem' (17-year-old Adem Crosby has been diagnosed with leukaemia for the second time since last February). Now, during presentations in a park at Inverell, Alex told other riders of Adem's battles and his planned ride in support.

Then it was time for the random cash draws for the riders who completed their own personal challenge—20 draws at $100 each. At around the fifth draw, Matt Muir, a cyclist from Yamba, won $100. He accepted the prize then immediately handed it over to Alex to go to Team Adem. Then every following prizewinner and the previous ones got up and donated their prizes to Alex. To top it off, two generous riders, donated a further $1000.

Alex so swelled with pride, he burst into tears after his fellow riders raised $3000 in ten minutes.

If you see a chance . . .

A reader had just put his car into his newly built garage—finished that day—when the mother and father of all hailstorms broke and proceeded to wipe out every tiled roof for miles around.

'I stood and watched the mayhem from the cover of the new garage,' he recounts, 'and after a short while, Bronte Road was about six inches deep from one side of the road to the other and from top to bottom . . . All of a sudden a car load of young guys pulled up on the footpath, surveyed the scene. Yes, I thought, these guys are all struck by the power of nature. They are conscious of the damage, the disrupted lives, the people who will be sleeping to the slapping sound of tarpaulins for months to come.

'But no! They were checking it out! Surveying it, like a climber picks his route or a surfer checks the surf. Out of the boot came three boogie boards and with excited whoops they hit the slopes, at pace, yahooing all the way.'

DRIVE
ELEGANTLY

All batsmen love going in on a road

Late last Saturday afternoon—a beautifully warm late spring day, just like mother used to make—a group of 14-year-old boys gathered at a mate's place at Cronulla to celebrate his birthday. They were playing cricket on his quiet suburban street. But wait. A car is slowly approaching.

Momentarily, the boys stop and remove the garbage bin wickets from the road and allow the driver through so he can get to his home a few blocks down. The driver cheerily waves as he passes, and one of the kids asks if he'd like to have a hit with them? Sure enough, a few minutes later, after the driver has parked and said hello to his missus, he ambles back and spends the next half-hour batting, bowling and joking with the kids.

When he finally says farewell, he leaves behind a bunch of kids absolutely gobsmacked about who they'd actually been playing street cricket with. Well done, Ricky Ponting.

Mona Vale mudlarks

In August, an under-12 rugby league grand final for the ages was played between the young lads of Mona Vale and Belrose at Curl Curl's Reub Hudson Oval. The Mona Vale boys gave it their best, but the nippers from Belrose were just that little bit stronger.

No matter, it was a great game, made all the better by the fact that just before full-time, a young bloke from Mona Vale scored a consolation try right in the corner where a fabulous mud puddle lay, covering himself from head to foot in wonderful goo. And are you thinking what I'm thinking? You are!

At the final whistle, instead of doing a customary lap of honour, the Belrose boys decided they wanted to have the same fun as the Mona Vale try-scorer and, almost as one, ran to the same mud puddle and dived in. Then all the Mona Vale boys joined them, dragging their coach as they went.

Finally, the piece de resistance. Stand back everyone—here he comes! For now it is the referee himself, aged 40 or so, racing down the sideline—as all the parents clap and cheer—before taking a flying leap and landing in the middle of the muddy, laughing throng!

Now, which boys are Belrose, which ones are from Mona Vale, who are the winners and losers and what was the score of the grand final again? It just doesn't matter. Kids' sport, exactly as it should be—and three cheers for the ref.

Trek stars

Last weekend, aided by guides, four vision-impaired members of the Achilles Running Club trekked 50 kilometres in the Coastrek Challenge, from Palm Beach to Balmoral, to raise money for the Fred Hollows Foundation. Setting out from Palm Beach in heavy rain and a driving head wind at 6.20am on Friday morning, they arrived 18½ gruelling hours later, to the rapturous applause of almost nobody.

They congratulated each other, tended their blisters and then quietly went on their way. Magnificent!

♪♫ With a ball
in my goal ... ♪♫

Sing and you're winning

One morning, about five years ago, Ben Shine was sitting at a sports ground in the inner city waiting for his soccer grand final to start, and passing the time by watching one of the curtain-raiser games, between two under-9 teams.

'The first half,' he writes, 'was a tense affair with parents and other onlookers screaming their lungs out at these kids, and it was obvious that this grand final meant a lot to them. The first half ended 2–0 to the blue team, and as I was lucky enough to be sitting next to the losing team of Abbotsford, I overheard their coach give their half-time pep talk.

'Instead of the usual "play it up the guts", "give 110 per cent" speech, the coach's speech consisted entirely of an enthusiastic rendition of "If you're happy and you know it". It was obvious that this coach, who had a strong Greek accent, cared only about the kids being happy and not the result of the game, unlike many of the parents.

'Anyway, the Abbotsford team went out in the second half and proceeded to score three unanswered goals, thus winning the game, sending the team and the coach back into another chorus of "If you're happy and you know it". It was an amazing sight, and I only wish I had a coach like that.'

Small world

A Queenslander by the name of Dave McPhillips was invited to attend a black-tie wedding at Palm Beach. But, wouldn't you bloody know it? When he arrives at Sydney Airport he realises he's left his suit pants at home! And the wedding is in *90 minutes*.

Quickly picking up his hire car, the whole way from Mascot to the wedding he looks out for a shop that hires or sells formal pants, only to find diddly-squat. He is nearly at Palm Beach, and completely desperate when he spies an older bloke, around about his size, mowing his front lawn.

It is time to play his last card. Pulling over, he explains his situation, and that he has only 15 minutes to spare.

'Hmmm. What did you say your name was?'

'Dave McPhillips.'

'Any relation to the McPhillips who played outside-centre for Queensland in 1962–63?'

'My uncle!'

'I was his inside-centre.'

And, by the way, of course he can have the pants regardless of the rugby connection. And they fit like a glove. Dave rushes off to make the wedding just in time, and everyone lives happily ever after, including the beautiful bride who walks down the aisle, untroubled by any dickhead in the back row wearing jeans on the formal occasion which is her big day.

Serves and snaps

Steve Healy was at the Davis Cup final two weeks ago* and observed an interesting scene. Courtside there were many boxes, including the President's Reserve, which was packed with heavies such as Prime Minister John Howard and his wife Jeanette, Victorian Premier Steve Bracks, and Lachlan Murdoch and his wife Sarah O'Hare. Two bays along sat the 'The Fanatics', as the Australian supporter team call themselves, gaily bedecked in all their green 'n' gold T-shirts and the like and putting out an endless series of chants.

'Halfway through the afternoon, as the tennis battle raged,' Healy recounts, 'one of the young supporters wandered over to the President's Reserve armed with a camera and approached Lachlan Murdoch and his wife Sarah O'Hare'. By this time most of the 14,000 crowd was watching. Much to everybody's amusement they saw the supporter put one arm over Lachlan's shoulder and the other over Sarah's, while Steve Bracks took a photo of them.

He then proceeded down to the front row to meet the PM and his wife. As a game was just about to resume, Mr Howard indicated he should wait until the next change of ends and the supporter sat down in a vacant seat next to Bracks and had a chat. Sure enough, at the next change of ends the supporter had his photo taken with the PM, again by Bracks.

Security calmly observed this and the crowd gave him a big cheer as he returned to the Fanatics. How many countries of the world could you do that in?

*Australia v. France at the Rod Laver Arena, Melbourne, 30 November–2 December, 2001; France victorious 3–2

City has a heart

Last week, a bloke by the name of Hamish Fraser had what he describes as 'the great privilege' of riding his push bike—bearing a large flag—just ahead of the sole wheelchair competitor in the Sydney half marathon: a bloke by the name of Pion, from South Korea.

After a handshake, a nod of thanks and a couple of scattered words of English, off they go, just a couple of minutes ahead of the runners. With his arms pumping like pistons, Pion especially put in on the arduous hill sections.

The lovely thing? As most runners passed Pion going up the hill, they found the energy to give him some warm applause, or words of encouragement. But as Pion reached the halfway point and turned around it *really* got going.

Now all the runners still behind Hamish and Pion in the race were in an adjacent lane racing *towards* them, and our man on the bike reports that 'almost to a person, the runners going the other way yelled, cheered or clapped Pion. The effect for the two of us alone was that for about three kilometres, we enjoyed this wave of cheering like nothing I've ever experienced. I don't know if it helped Pion along, but it made me feel a little choked up!'

No ball!

Barrackers to the fore

'One morning, a couple of weeks ago, as I was jogging along New South Head Road in Double Bay, I idly thought that with the cricket season approaching . . . I'd break up the pounding rhythm of the run by practising my bowling run-up, delivery stride and rolling of the arm thereover. Just as I was through my third delivery a bloke leaned from the passenger seat of a speeding removals van and yelled, "Howizzeeeee!?!", as blokes leaning from [said vehicles] are wont to do.

'Last Thursday lunchtime, I was jogging again, this time along the Harbour Bridge heading towards North Sydney for a swim— and again I was into bowling practice. Just as I was through what might've been a pretty good fast-medium offering, a guy yelled from the passenger seat of another van, "No ball!!!" and I gave pause to reflect: what a great country we live in.

'Soon after, though, the peach: as I approached the steps which lead down to Kirribilli, an old digger, a man who'd seen better days, who'd obviously been studying my imaginary thunderbolts, looked me up and down, and said, "Who the f@&# are you? F@&#in' Warney?"'

Three's a rarity

Last week Ascham's 2nds softball team got three of their Roseville opponents out on one ball—a triple play. One reader calculated: 'They only occur about three or four times a season in the Major League American competition. That's 30 teams playing in 162 games each team per season . . . bear with me . . . at a minimum of nine innings each game . . . at least three at bats each innings for each team . . . running out of fingers here . . . so each team has 4374 minimum at bats per season and with 30 teams, that's about 131,200 per year. And last season, there were THREE triple plays!'

Redfern rescue

Our curtain opens on a scene last Tuesday at high noon on Redfern train station. Two Anglo-Saxson mothers are seriously struggling with their prams as they try to alight from a train that is about to take off.

Quick as a flash an Indian student and a Middle-Eastern tradie rush to help, each lifting a pram.

A Mediterranean grandma calls out to the Asian train guard to hold the train and the whole operation ends happily.

Other commuters even look up from their mobile phones, interacting with each other, and smiled.

Reg

All the marbles

A nice kind of bloke is Kingswood sewing machine repairman Terry Rastall, even if he has lost his marbles. But already I am ahead of myself . . .

See, just three weeks ago, Terry had a call from a woman from Haberfield wanting her machine repaired, giving an address that he immediately recognised as the childhood home he and his family had moved from 40 years earlier. As he entered the premises, the years fell away. Those long hot summers! The other neighbourhood kids! The fun in the backyard!

Ah, yes, the backyard. Back then, Terry had been *the* hotshot marble player in the neighbourhood and so loved the game, and was so good that he had collected close on 500 marbles, his prize possession. Some said he was the best in the whole suburb, maybe the whole city!

And now, in conversation with the woman of the house, Terry admits his principal regret in leaving this old place was the fact that on the day of departure, his naughty brother had grabbed all these marbles and spread them all over the backyard!

Funny he should say that. The nice lady brightens up and says that for the past 40 years, while toiling in the garden, hanging out the washing and all the rest, she has been finding, cleaning and collecting those marbles and . . . keeping them in a container in the laundry!

Would Terry like them back? He would! Excitedly, Terry takes the precious container home, and counts them up—342 of the beauties!

But the story gets better still. For when he tells his mate the story, those mates tell him about the Australian Marbles Championships coming up in Brunswick Heads soon. Terry decides to take on the challenge with his old marbles, starts practising, then travels up for the tournament.

And all the old skills come back. Winning round after round, he makes it all the way to the three-game final and then takes the title from four-time winner Andrew Hanlon, two games to one. He is now, officially, the best marbles player in all of *Australia*.

Strike a chord

Earlier this year, Judy Gowland was going through her son's bedroom when she came across his tenor saxophone and clarinet, rarely used since his days back in the high school jazz band. Remembering an article she'd seen in the paper a few months ago about the Granville Boys High School band needing instruments, she rang the school to ask if they would like her son's instrument, to which the principal, Linda O'Brien, replied, 'Would we what!'

The school has 500 students, 99 per cent of whom come from non-English speaking backgrounds, and has its challenges. In short order, Judy visited the school, met the student who now has a top range saxophone (Ahmed Osman of Year 9), and became the patron of the GBHS concert band.

Sign of the times

It was 1pm on a Saturday in May, up at the Koola ovals at Killara. On one field there was a classic suburban rugby game with the local lads giving some equally rough 'n' ready 'n' rotund visitors a pretty solid work-over. On the next field was a UTS women's soccer game. Then came the rain and the wind. Who knew what kind of storm was about to blow up? Just to be sure, the rugby lads ran for shelter. The women played on, one of them receiving a yellow card for unnecessary roughness.

Bondi remembers

Maybe you missed it, but the following letter appeared in the *Sydney Morning Herald* letters page on Monday.*

> I've just experienced something remarkable. I went down to Bondi Beach just before midday, breaking off a twig of bottlebrush along the way as a mark of respect to those poor folk in Bali. It was an average, sunny Sydney day.
>
> As I walked on to the sand at North Bondi the shark siren fired up and every person on the beach, man, woman and child, stood up and faced the sea. There was complete silence. After a minute the siren sounded again and people went back to doing their Sunday beach thing.
>
> It was at once beautiful, chilling and singularly Australian. I will never forget it.
>
> Brendan Gallagher,
> Bondi

*20 October 2002, eight days after the Bali Bombings

"Unconfirmed leak from undisclosed sauce..."

PIE BITES MAN

Only in Oz . . .

From reader Greg Eccleston: 'Cricketer takes a banned diet pill, sent home from a tour'—front-page story, pages two and three (in another paper). 'Australians being sent on a tour of duty, PM meets US President, global war imminent'—page four. Gawd, I love this country!!!

Briefs on wheels

And after the fortnight of shocking news we've just had,* you'll excuse me if I maintain that right now aces are high, jacks are low, and every feel-good story we can muster are trumps. With that in mind, Hugh Dillon, who is a magistrate, shares this anecdote:

'I was walking along Elizabeth Street showing some young German lawyers the legal district. We were chatting away about our different legal cultures. As we yak away, a barrister (with the usual barrister paraphernalia) flies past on a skateboard . . .'

*Following the Bali Bombings

Messages from above and below

Up Brisbane way, Cameron McDonald reports: 'I was going for a swim when I saw that a bird had "visited" the bonnet of my car. I thought I'd do my laps first and then clean it off. But when I returned . . . and this is true . . . someone else had done it for me!'

Go Alex Graham!

Bravo, Hornsby RSL Soccer Club. I heard a yarn this week about the mother of a seven-year-old boy with severe cerebral palsy, who had approached a few clubs to see if her son could join them and play in some fashion. The kid was sports mad, in part because he has seen his three older sisters play sport over the years. As his parents, they were keen that he experience something of what it is to belong to a team—to attend training, make friends, play the games, know the joy of victory and the disappointment of defeat.

Could their boy perhaps join them, even though he couldn't run, and to get around at all he needed a walking frame? The answers came back: No. No. No. No. Then she approached the Hornsby RSL Soccer Club, and the answer was immediate: Yes, of course!

Young Alex Graham now attends training with all the other boys and girls on a Wednesday night, does the drills the best he can, listens to the coach, has the drinks break when he says, and then gets back into it. To make it easier for Alex, the club has provided him with a smaller ball so that when he kicks his foot under the front of the frame, it is easier for him to reach.

Though of normal intelligence, Alex cannot talk like the other kids, but the word is that if his constant face-splitting smiles were translated to words he would be saying 'Hurrah! Hurrah! HURRAH!'

People passion

Half-time in the Bledisloe Cup, NZ ahead 23–8. Jake Elliott was there. The crowd had been stunned into silence by the All Blacks onslaught. In the stands, two young men stood shoulder to shoulder, arm in arm as the Wallabies jogged off the field. Without a word, they both knew what needed to be done. They needed to evade the masses pushing towards the bars and the loos and sneak into the more refined members' area.

And a nice kind of gents it was too when they got there, if packed. Funny though, there wasn't a sound coming from this morose mob. It was too much to bear so one of the young blokes shouted out: 'What is going on? Why is everyone so quiet? There is still a half to go! The game's not over! Where is your spirit? What we need to do is sing!'

Silence. And then a lone voice from the other side of the bathroom replied: 'I'll sing with you!'

The first bloke asked 'What's your name, mate?'

'Stefan,' was the answer.

'What do you want to sing, Stefan?'

'I don't know mate, you decide.'

A slight pause, and then the bloke started off, 'Once a jolly swagman camped by a billabong' before the rest of the assembly joined in, 'UNDER THE SHADE OF A COOLIBAH TREE!' And all the previously morose sang a booming and hopeful chorus of 'Waltzing Matilda'.

Possum magic

Diana Southwell-Keely was walking with her husband back to their car near Hyde Park when they saw a possum on the road which was clearly distressed and disoriented, lurching almost drunkenly into the traffic and then back onto the footpath, before tripping forward again. Everyone stopped, stared and wondered what to do.

There! An ambulance on its way to Sydney Hospital in Macquarie Street suddenly pulled up. Out got an ambulance officer, calmly retrieved a blanket from the back, grabbed the possum, wrapped it up and put it in the back of the van, before driving off. Presumably, to the possum hospital.

Father and son in thriller

Exactly 20 years ago the *Sydney Morning Herald* noted how the St Pat's Sutherland men's cricket team had come last or second-last in the comp for 11 seasons in a row. Well, the nucleus of that team is still together, led by Mark Monaghan and Adam Young with 34 years and 35 years of consecutive service respectively. Now, with their sons Andrew, 17, and Chris, 14, having joined, it gives the team an age range of 14–54 years.

Last weekend in the semi-final they played Como, who set a very competitive total of 244. After a great innings by batsmen McGuirk and Merceica of 97 and 70 respectively, the ninth wicket fell in the second-last over with St Pat's still needing three runs to win.

Mark Monaghan—who used to be a goodish batsman until his eyesight went on him—strides out to join his son, Andrew, in the middle. Andrew is on strike and smashes two past point to tie the game, with one over to go. Mark is now on strike and blocks the first five deliveries. One ball to play. Finally he removes his optical sunglasses and gives them to the umpire. 'Hold these please ump, they're very disorienting.' The bowler runs in, the fieldsmen press, Mark sights the ball, puts his foot down the wicket and swings . . . connection!

The ball crashes through the covers, allowing father and son to run two as the huge St Pat's crowd—about 25, maybe as many as 30—go berserk. Clapping away quietly in the middle of the euphoric group was one very proud 85-year-old woman, Nancy, Mark's mother and Andrew's grandmother. And Como were great sports about it all too.

Commuters' hang up

The scene was set last Thursday morning, just after a train packed with commuters leaves Milsons Point station to head over the Sydney Harbour Bridge and into the city. Suddenly the voice of a train guard, with timbre and enunciation that could make John Laws nod his head with appreciation, rolls from the speakers in every carriage.

'Good morning, passengers. It's a beautiful day and you are now crossing the most magnificent harbour in the world. So why don't you look up from your phones and enjoy the view. You won't get a better attraction for the price of a train ticket.'

And some of them even did!

Energy savers

This bloke—let's call him Big Jack—goes for a swim on Christmas Day at Manly Beach, and is standing on a sandbank in chest-deep water when a sudden surge sweeps his feet out from under him, to take him seawards in a strong rip! Not panicking, but swimming hard, of course, he looks to the shore, where he can see the lifesavers watching him intently and . . . chatting earnestly. But not actually doing anything.

Still not panicking, he keeps swimming hard until, finally, exhausted, his feet touch the sand again . . . only to be swept away once more! Same thing: he looks to the shore, and there are the lifesavers, all with their eyes on him, talking animatedly, and one or two pointing in his direction. And . . . stroke. And . . . stroke. And . . . stroke. One more time, his feet touch the bottom, and this time he gets purchase and manages to stagger to the shore where he sinks to the sunny sand.

A shadow falls across him. He looks up. There are the lifesavers. They have a six-pack of beer with them. 'Mate,' one of them says, giving him the six-pack, 'we were taking bets on whether we would have to come out and rescue you. You deserve this.'

A pair of young champions in the making

It's a school cross country race. The usual winner of the senior girls division, Caitlin Hickey, had left her opponents so far behind they were in a different postcode, only to suddenly pull up badly lame with 400 metres to go.

All she can do is hobble forward to the finishing line, and she is just 50 metres off when her great friend and rival Jasmine Nix catches her.

'What's up?'

'My toe is broken and I can't run.'

Jasmine offers to walk the last part of the race with her and such is their lead they approach the tape with still no other runners close.

Five metres off, Jasmine offers first place to her friend, reasoning that, but for the broken toe, Caitlin would have finished well in front.

Champions both. Caitlin declines and insists her friend deserves the win. So they agree to break the tape together, but at the last instant Caitlin pauses and sends her friend over first to take the win.

The other stadium

It was the wee hours of Sunday morning.* There was madness in the air as the celebrations and commiserations went on. One of our readers wandered onto a platform at Central station in what was usually the silent watch of the night to find a bunch of blokes in gold jerseys and a bunch in black, playing a catch-as-catch-can game of rugger, complete with rucks, mauls and lineouts, and having the time of their lives.

*22 November 2003, a week after the Wallabies' famous victory over the All Blacks in the semis at the Rugby World Cup

54

Security not so alert

On Sunday afternoon, reader Allan Marsden was driving past the private jet terminal at Kingsford-Smith Airport when he noticed the sleek lines of the United States Air Force jet that had just brought Secretary of State John Kerry and Defence Secretary Chuck Hagel here for their visit. Being something of an aviation buff *and* a stickybeak, he stops the car, and walks up to the security fence . . . only to see a police car pull up a couple of minutes later.

Oh . . . Gawd.

Is he about to be arrested?

The cop gets out. Walks up to him. Takes out his camera.

Starts taking photos.

Of the plane.

'Ummm,' says our man, 'I thought I would be arrested doing that?'

'Why?' says the cop, bemused. 'It is only a plane?'

Gotta love this country!

Under the tough exterior beats a heart of gold

This week I heard the story of a bloke who attended the rugby World Cup semi between Australia and New Zealand with his seven-year-old son, only to find they were in seats right in front of the most enormous Maori man he'd ever seen, replete with tattoos, black singlet and a tray of beers on his lap. Surrounded by all his mates!

The Australian—intimidated and fearing he knew not what—pulled his son close and mumbled his way through the Australian national anthem as a way of not drawing attention to himself. The son would have none of it, though, and bellowed out the words with everything he had in him. 'ADVANCE AUSTRALIA FAIRRRRRRR!'

Oh no. The Maori is now leaning forward to tap his son on the shoulder. The Australian is now tense all over, just about everywhere but his sphincter.

'Son,' the Maori says, 'that was the bust singing of any anffem I have eva heard at any game I 'eva bin to. Here's two bucks. Go buy yerself an ice-cream.'

Catch of the season

It's a soft, summery evening and a social softball competition is in progress. The teams are of various stripes, with many sides taking it all waaay too seriously—you know who you are. But the standout team is made up of players and their carers from the Lachlan Centre, a live-in care facility for people with intellectual disabilities. The team ensures everyone on the side has an equal go and, last week, in the last game of the season, these Lachlan Tigers were playing the mighty Zoolanders in a tight one. You shoulda been there . . .

'Bottom of the fifth, bases loaded, two strikes down,' as we say in the trade, and a young woman from the Zoolanders swings with everything she's got and—you beauty!—hits the ball harder and higher than she has all season. Still, running back as hard as he can is a young Tiger called Mark. Can he catch it? If he can, it will be the first catch he has taken in his life but he is at least running with everything he has. Back, further back, as the crowd cheers encouragement, the ball is descending now, faster and faster. Back a little further, Mark, go, go, GO . . . he's going to miss it altogether . . . no, he's going to be under it! . . . he puts out a glove . . . it's in . . . he's GOT IT!

Now both teams crowd around him in congratulations, led by the young Zoolander who has just had her home run thwarted.

To top it off, in the final innings, every member of the entire Tigers squad made home runs—about 30 of them—whereupon both teams huddled for the respective three cheers and then a walk-past of handshakes and high fives.

Paper trail ends here

The scene is set in downtown Sydney last Monday lunchtime. The wind roars through the concrete canyons of Sydney . . . up Sussex Street, right on to Market Street and down George Street before bursting into Martin Place . . . just as a busy business-man on the phone is scurrying to his next appointment. And watch now as the wicked wind tugs at the cover of the bag he is wheeling behind him, an instant before a whole sheaf of papers come whirling out to be scattered all around the Cenotaph, as he keeps walking . . . oblivious.

Sydney swings into action. A grandmotherly figure in her runners sprints off after him to get his attention while at the same time—with no-one saying anything—a dozen passersby includ-ing office workers, fellow business-people, tourists, a student and some retirees all stomp their feet down on the papers as they fly past. The businessman returns, thanking everyone as they remove the papers from under their footwear and hand them all back to him.

Job done. Everyone moves on.

Get that up yer!

A well-known member of the Australian women's rugby team turned out for Warringah's fifth-grade side against Southern Districts. Apparently her opponent was unimpressed and reportedly made less-than-polite remarks about how women had no business playing rugby.

Our heroine waited till the bloke came at her with ball in hand and cut him in two with a tackle that would have felled a rhinoceros. And again and again. The coach was eventually forced to move him to a different position to get him away from her.

Listen, you misogynous mongrels: what part of 'we women rugby players will NOT be denied access to a game that WE own, too!' don't you understand?!

The Strange Case of

Dr Jeckyll and Frank Hyde

Frank Hyde rekindles league's glowing heart

Last Saturday arvo, two of rugby league's foundation clubs, the Newtown Jets and North Sydney Bears, are battling to win the Frank Hyde Shield at Henson Park. At half-time, after 40 minutes of torrid but entertaining football, the Jets are holding a narrow lead.

The great Frank Hyde himself, who started playing for Newtown in 1934, before going to play with Norths, is presented to the crowd from the commentary position, and the people cheer. The octogenarian is nearing the end of a wonderful speech of reminiscences when someone in the crowd yells out: 'Danny Boy!'

Hyde pauses, looks a little misty, gazes down on the crowd and replies softly: 'Would you like to hear 'Danny Boy', would you?' They certainly would.

Out on the breeze then, across field over the crowd and beyond, comes a hauntingly beautiful rendition of 'Danny Boy'. And, now, I want readers to hum it with him as the great man sings:

Oh Danny boy, the pipes, the pipes are calling;
From glen to glen, and down the mountain side
The summer's gone, and all the flowers are dying;
'Tis you, 'tis you must go and I must bide
But come ye back when summer's in the meadow;

Or when the valley's hushed and white with snow
'Tis I'll be here in sunshine or in shadow;
Oh Danny boy, oh Danny boy, I love you so . . .

Stunning. You see? Flickering, maybe, but that wondrous torch
of league-as-it-was still burns! Newtown went on to beat Norths
42–20 to win the cup.

Good old patience

You have to picture the scene, one set of traffic lights back from a busy expressway on Tuesday afternoon last. Before the red light, in the thick traffic, the mood is tired and frustrated as everyone aches to get going, get on the expressway and head for home. When will the bloody thing turn green? And, hang on, what is this?

An elderly man with a walking frame starts to cross the six lanes with exceedingly slow and painful steps, and is only halfway across when the traffic lights do indeed turn green. The mood instantly changes. This man is a representative of our parents' generation, when things were kinder, gentler, more chivalrous. What was that thing they told us about patience, again? 'Patience is a virtue, possess it if you can. Seldom in a woman, never in a man.'

On this occasion, however, everyone displays it, and as the old fellow continues to make his way across, there is not one toot heard, not one *peep*, out of anyone, and even on the near-side well away from him, not one car moves until he has safely reached the footpath on the far side.

Shire brilliance

The following are excerpts from a genuine match report, written by a 'Che Guevara' from the Shire*, recounting a visit made by the Burraneer under-13s team to play the silvertails of the eastern suburbs.

'You drive your Ford halfway across the city and park it amongst all the BMWs and Range Rovers under some magnificent old Moreton Bay figs. You get out of the car and walk into a rugby club the size of a small town. You stand outside, surrounded by the beautiful people wearing their power clothes, fresh from their trip to the health spa or Friday lunch. And whilst paying a fortune for your beer, you watch your children get hammered by GIANTS.

I know everything is supposed to be bigger and better in tinseltown . . . but has it got to extend to 13-year-old boys playing rugby??? Now I only have a few things to report . . .

Not everything in life has a happy ending and this is one of those times. People say size isn't everything. Well, that's crap when you're playing rugby.

We all like to win but everyone can't. You learn from your losses—but it hurts.

Listen to what people tell you—but only if it's useful.

And finally; even though we got hammered and we had to go to Café Latte Land to cop the beating, remember this:

you can take all the gold Amex cards and BMW cars and trips to the beauty parlour and overpriced brand-name clothing, pretentious accents and Moreton Bay figs, and stick 'em right where the sun don't shine. Because you guys play for Burraneer and . . . YOU LIVE IN THE SHIRE!!!!!!!'

Right on! I love that.

*The Shire is famous for its beaches, its surf culture, its fierce localism and as the home of *Puberty Blues*

Good shot, that

A reader reports that summer must be on the way because the first blowfly has entered the house and is driving him nuts. That's as may be, but summer won't truly be in the air until the dulcet tones of Richie Benaud fill the airwaves and the first warning is put in the papers that 'the state is a tinderbox'.

Team effort

Early last week the first grade Sydney Uni Hockey Club player Chris Pelow, an Irishman, consulted a mate of his in fifth grade about his crook right foot. That mate, health professional Damo Cunningham, immediately sensed it was serious and steered him towards the radiographer in first grade, Dougal Alexander, who promptly guided Pelow through a series of scans and MRIs, which showed a real problem. This looked like a job for Sanjeev Gupta, an orthopedic surgeon who used to play first grade for the club and now plays masters.

On Tuesday night, at training, the still calm Pelow told his teammates the upshot: he had been diagnosed with a synovial sarcoma, a rare but vicious cancer, and the only treatment was to have his lower leg amputated to prevent it spreading. That was going to happen on the morrow.

Two men to whom this was no news were SUHC club captain Mark Crennan and first grade coach Chris Moylan—as they had already taken the week off their jobs to help, and this included organising to fly Pelow's parents from Ireland and accommodating them. Many others in the club helped in their own way.

The amputation went ahead, and the early signs are good. As noted by the report on the club's website: 'No one wants a crisis. If there is one, SUHC is up to it.'

Ask a stupid, stupid question . . .

Decla Baxter was commuting from Tempe to her job in North Sydney, she tells me. 'I'd finished reading the morning paper and was saving it to bring to friends on the job. So how do you save a newspaper on State Rail? You sit on it!! A new commuter came in, saw the newspaper under my rear end and asked the second most stupid question I've ever heard: "Are you reading that paper?" I stood up, turned the page, sat right back down on the paper and answered . . . "Yes."'

What price silence?

The place: Woolworths, Marrickville Metro, 11.59 am Sunday 23 January 2005. An announcement comes over the public address system requesting a minute's silence for the tsunami victims. As one, every shopper stops shopping, and every trolley stops rolling.

The total silence lasts for all of five seconds before another announcement comes from, clearly, another microphone, well removed from the announcement: 'PRICE CHECK AISLE THREE … BRIAN, CAN WE GET A PRICE CHECK IN AISLE THREE PLEASE?'

The rainbow after the storm

Mark Hurley, his wife and two young sons went camping last weekend, only to be beaten by the howling wind and torrential rain. The upside to the misadventure was the chance to be back in the Big Smoke for the grand final and, as keen Canterbury Bulldogs supporters, they decided the best place to soak some of the atmosphere would be in the park next to Telstra Stadium.

Twenty minutes before kick-off, the family was approached by two friendly looking blokes offering them four free tickets to the game, as their friends had not shown up. They didn't want any money, Hurley says, but suggested they make a donation to charity. Thus, the Hurleys were seated next to the spot where the Bulldogs scored their two second-half tries.

Great moments in sport:
Italy please take note

Because last week's big wet forced a last-minute change of venue, the Mosman Football Club under-10 soccer team arrived at the new field for the game against Narrabeen with only eight players. Not to worry, Narrabeen offered three of theirs, and the game began.

The three players offered proved to be crackers who played their hearts out and scored the only two goals for the Mosman side. At game's end—a lovely 2–2 draw—both teams cheered and carried the recruited goalscorers from the field on their shoulders. Each team then nominated a player from the other side as their man of the match.

Every parent, after mingling and chatting with the parents of the opposing team, walked away from the field with their arm around their child and a smile as wide as the Sydney Harbour Bridge, knowing that this was really what sport was meant to be all about in the first place.

Hugh Jackman, the real wizard of Oz

We now cross to one of the most influential columnists in America, Dominick Dunne of *Vanity Fair*, a man who can make or break a career in a single column item. Take it away, Dom . . .

'I went to the Imperial Theatre for the closing matinee performance of *The Boy From Oz*, starring the great Hugh Jackman, in possibly the most dazzling male performance in a musical in the history of Broadway. The final performance was a show business love-fest, the likes of which I had never seen in a lifetime of theatregoing. The cheering started as soon as the curtain rose; I lost track of the standing ovations Jackman received in the course of the performance. This guy dominates the stage in the same way Ethel Merman used to, and he clearly loves his audience as much as they love him.'

Jackman's first time on the stage was in first class at Pymble Public in 1974, when he was in the chorus of *The Wizard Of Oz* beside lifelong friend Angus Worland. 'I actually thought I was better than him,' Worland laughed, 'but then in year 9 at Knox, when we did the musical *How To Succeed In Business Without Really Trying*, I think he started to pull ahead.'

How far he's come . . .

Shhhhh! Manly have scored!

Last Saturday night the Sportsman's Bar at the Dee Why RSL, right in the middle of Manly territory, was chock-a-block with punters watching the telecast of the Manly Sea Eagles–Canterbury Bulldogs match, beamed lived from the Olympic stadium. The beer was flowing and from the opening whistle it was obvious that for the first time in nine years the Sea Eagles were fair dinkum competing! Never mind that Canterbury scored first, Manly struck back quickly with a try of their own and . . .

'And, ladies and gentlemen,' a voice comes over the speakers, 'would you please all rise, for a moment's silence, to observe the tradition in RSL clubs across the land, while the *Ode of Remembrance* is recited.'

The lights are dimmed as the TV is turned to mute and, as one, all of the punters do indeed rise and put down their beers, standing to a rough attention facing the screen.

'They shall grow not old, as we that are left grow old.'

(Now Manly are *again* heading towards the Bulldogs' line.)

'Age shall not weary them, nor the years condemn.'

(They're flicking the ball around like the Harlem Globetrotters! Still not a peep has escaped the punters, even through the rising excitement.)

'At the going down of the sun and in the morning . . .'

(They're getting close! Just 10 metres out now! TRY! TRY! TRY! Not one sound has escaped them, though.)

'*We will remember them . . . We will remember them.*'

The lights come back up, and then, and only then, do the Manly supporters give full vent to their joy, with people cheering, jumping up on chairs and pumping their fists.

Kiss and tell

In how many other nations around the world would we have witnessed the wonderful scene at the end of the 2007 A-League grand final during the trophy ceremony? I refer to the moment when after John Howard gave a victor's medallion to Melbourne Victory's Kristian Sarkies, the young midfielder—overcome with the euphoria of it all—leaned forward and with a broad smile planted a wet kiss atop the prime ministerial pate.

The response was not a dozen security guards wrestling him to the ground, bitter criticism for interfering with the PM's august person, or anything of the kind. The Prime Minister merely gave a sheepish, if slightly stunned, grin, and normal programming was quickly resumed. Loved it.

Where Eagles care

Dalwood House is a Department of Education and Department of Health centre, catering for up to a dozen rural students at a time with literacy problems. A reader's 10-year-old son, Bill, has been staying there for a short spell, and though the regime is relatively strict—no direct contact with parents except for two telephone calls a week, and no visitors—progress in literacy has been steady.

Still, homesickness was something of a problem for the young lad, and to try to alleviate it, the reader and her husband rang a family friend whose son goes to school with the son of Manly football coach Des Hasler; she asked if there was any way the Sea Eagles could organise tickets for the kids to watch last Friday night's game.

Done. Last Thursday, Mrs Hasler arrived at Dalwood House with the 12 tickets for the kids and their two lucky house parents—and a good time was subsequently had by all. Try as they might, the lads' parents in Forbes couldn't see young Bill in the crowd on the tele, but they are very appreciative of the Haslers' kindness.

Flying the flag

Over the summer break, the most momentous sporting event was, of course, the highly controversial Sydney Test,* which Australia won in extremis. On the first day of that Test, an interesting scene took place on the southern concourse.

One of my spies reports that at one stage, a small boy of obviously Indian birth, with a sky-blue Sahara shirt on, made his way to the fence, tightly clutching a pen and a small Indian flag. With equal parts purpose and hope, he hung both over the fence in the direction of the Indian player Yuvraj Singh, who was fielding nearby. Alas, Singh totally ignored him.

The crowd then took the boy's part, booing the Indian player, before taking up the chant: 'Sign the flag, sign the flag.' *Still* no response!

At this point, a Sydneysider approached the lad and handed him an Australian flag, in the manner of 'You might do better with this, sonny', which drew the response of laughs all around, including from the lad.

Eventually, Singh's spot was taken by Sourav Ganguly.

Again, the crowd chanted 'Sign the flag, sign the flag!', and booed when he seemed to refuse. In fact, Ganguly was just waiting for the right opportunity, and signed the flag between overs.

To this, the crowd cheered, and then stood and bowed in obeisance, making Ganguly 'King of the Concourse' for the next couple of hours.

*This was the January 2008 Test between Australia and India that gained notoriety for a series of bad umpiring decisions and accusations of bad sportsmanship on both sides

A little tale to tug at your heartstrings

A reader sent me the following note, which she found blowing down her street. In big black letters on red paper, it looks to have been written by a 9- or 10-year-old: *To Bonnie, You have been a good best friend to me. You have been my bestest friend in the whole tire world. When we fight it don't count to our life it only counts when we are being bestest friends. From Billy.*

In printing it in my column, I urged reconciliation: 'Come on, Bonnie! Please give Billy another chance! He clearly didn't mean it, whatever it was, is really sorry and all of the rest of us would love to have a bestest friend as good and loyal as him in the whole tire world.'

The following week I heard from one of the parents, Ian, who wrote: 'We were surprised and delighted to read your column on Sunday with its small piece on that lovely letter from one bestest friend to another. Bonnie is my eight-year-old daughter and Billi is indeed her best friend but one crucial fact was lost in translation—Billi is also an eight-year-old girl. They became friends at pre-school and now at primary school they sit together in class, do gymnastics together and only very occasionally fall out. Whatever tiff provoked this letter was quickly forgiven and forgotten. They are, as you said, good and loyal friends and I hope they always will be.'

So do we!

Just a game

Last Sunday, they held the NSW District Netball Championships at Meadowbank, and after six hours of play in the pouring rain, officials started announcing the winners over the loudspeaker. Most teams, sodden and exhausted, just quietly came up and received their trophies. Not the victorious under-15 Ryde–Eastwood girls, who hit the stage in force as their captain commandeered the microphone.

'Thank you, thank you all,' she said. 'We'd just like to thank everybody, and I'd also like to say ... that I'm probably the prettiest girl in the team.'

Great hilarity all round.

Old school meets older protocol

Since forever, the Sydney Uni Law Ball has been about as white-bread an event as they come, as the champagne flows and a great sense of history hovers over distinguished poo-bahs in black ties and long gowns who can hardly spit over their shoulder without hitting a High Court judge or PM of the future in the eye.

At last Friday evening's event, however, something different. For the first time in its long history—for it is, of course, the oldest such institution in Australia—it had a Welcome to Country, this one presided over by a 65-year-old Aboriginal man, Mandy Dawes.

His message contained something of his story, that as the son of a white mother and black father he had spent some of his early years as part of the stolen generation, and the rest of it sleeping under a car in Redfern because landlords wouldn't rent to a mixed-race couple. This Law School, he said, was responsible for creating the system that for so long held Aboriginal people down, but the reason why I am welcoming you onto our land is because this school has the guts to invite me here; to try to put things to right and to prevent it from ever happening again. So welcome to country and let's have a party!

He was met with a standing ovation, tears and by his own admission 'the best night I ever had.' Bravo.

Maidens handicapped

Last Saturday afternoon as the champagne continued to flow free at Rosehill's Golden Slipper meet, the inevitable happened. The line to the ladies' loo got longer as their patience got shorter. Well bugger that for a joke. There was no queue at all to the men's, so the answer was obvious.

That is why, just after 3pm, 20 rather startled men looked up from the urinals to see a posse of well-dressed and well-behaved but busting women storm the barricades and head for the cubicles. Not a man complained, made a comment or gesture. They understood. Ladies, be our guests . . .

Power to the people

Meanwhile, in a perpendicular universe not so far away, a reader was recently walking through the York Street entry to Wynyard station at peak hour when he saw an apparently homeless man lying against the wall on the hard, tiled floor. While, sadly, this is a common sight, the difference about this man was that he was sending a text message on his mobile phone, which he was charging in a power point in the wall placed there for the benefit of the cleaners.

And not so far away again, in the Pitt Street mall, a young bloke was holding up a large sign offering 'Free Hugs', with apparently a few takers.

Beach bliss

Trudging to Shelly Beach on Sunday afternoon, after being obliged to leave their car kilometres away, reader Simon Trowell and his father finally arrive to find it packed to the gills and steaming hot—a family of four ants would have struggled to find a free patch of sand. But, what's this? In the distance, the sound of cats being strangled? No, it is a group of bagpipers at the northern end of the beach kicking off with a superb rendition of Flower of Scotland. Why, exactly?

Ah! Now appears a beaming and beautiful bride in traditional long white dress and her proud father—of course in a grey suit. And now the whole beach breaks into a huge round of applause as the two of them walk down the sandy aisle to where the groom and gathering awaits by the Pacific Ocean. Later, another huge round of applause as the wedding wraps up.

How quickly the game can turn

Last Saturday afternoon, the lads of the under-12 St Ives cricket team were playing against their Roseville rivals, and doing it tough. Chasing St Ives' total of 130, Roseville were right on top at 4-122 with three overs to bowl.

But wait! One wicket fell, and then another. And then, suddenly, another! From an easy romp home to victory, Roseville suddenly have a real fight on their hands and, in the way of these things, the sudden tension in the air stops passers-by in their tracks from as far as 200 metres away and brings them all to the edge of the field to see how it will play out.

One over left ... six balls to the promised land, one way or another, with Roseville having just five runs to get and three wickets in hand. The young lad with the honour of bowling that last over steams in, the Roseville batsman hits and risks a run and ... and is run out! Cheers and groans in equal measure ring out around the ground. The next Roseville batsman manages to ease things a little with a single, but then another wicket falls! People are now coming from everywhere to see what the commotion is.

After Roseville score another couple, there are two balls to go; Roseville has one wicket still in hand, needing three runs for victory. The young bowler runs in and delivers a ball that Andrew Symonds might have been proud of. Though game, the young Roseville batsman just misses it, to the sound of the death rattle behind. Bowled him! Game over.

The bowler, exhausted, joyous, collapses in the arms of his father, who has stormed the field with all the other parents. No one can believe it. St Ives has taken six wickets for six runs in 17 balls. And yet, though very disappointed, the Roseville captain seeks out the St Ives coach, looks him right in the eye as he shakes his hand and offers his sincere congratulations, before leading his team in three cheers for St Ives . . . who offer the same in kind.

Driving miss crazy

Early one Sunday morning in the chilly, pre-dawn light, the 184 bus left Spit Junction at 6.01am heading to the city, chokka with runners heading to the Sydney Morning Herald Half Marathon. Shivering with cold and nervous tension, there was a strong sense of camaraderie as the bus hauled them closer to their fate. That atmosphere suddenly disappeared, however, at the stop opposite the Oaks Hotel, when the bus driver refused entry to another runner as she was concerned about exceeding the maximum number of passengers allowed on the bus.

The runner became extremely distressed and began to cry, imploring the driver to allow her to join the others and sobbing that this was what she had been training for for months and there was no other bus to catch—and if she didn't get on, she would miss out. The driver stood firm, whereupon some of the runners on the bus intervened, imploring her to change her mind. *Still* the driver refused.

Then a young mother and her little girl rose from their seats and walked forward. The young mother had a few quiet words with the driver. She politely told her that the distressed young woman could take her place and she and her child would get off. The driver agreed.

So the young mother and toddler got off, into the freezing, dark morning at 6.10am, the deeply appreciative runner took her spot . . . and the whole bus burst into sustained applause for the result and for the extreme generosity of the young woman to a stranger.

That's an unlucky streak

It was a typical late spring Friday evening at Paddington Bowling Club last week. A mixture of locals and stray workers were sipping their $4 'chardys' in the dappled light when suddenly a male person, of Caucasian appearance, ran at a fair clip in a westerly direction across greens three and two, while not wearing any clothes—I believe, yer 'onner, they're commonly referred to as 'streakers'—then jumped the fence onto the street.

This looked like a job for the long arm of the law. Standing in for them was the club's security guard who chased after him. Not long behind, was a convoy of three police cars and a paddy-wagon, which screamed to a halt, disgorging officers who joined the hunt.

My informant wonders if the streaker was a local who, now that he can't do it at the nearby SCG in front of 70,000 people—where he would face a $5500 fine and lifetime ban—is reduced to doing it at the Paddo Bowls in front of 100 people, thinking he is far from any penalty. Well, by God, if so, our streaker had another think coming!

Mosman glory

Last year TFF ran an item calling for players to be part of a soccer team made up of 17- to 23-year-olds suffering from Asperger's to play in the Warringah competition under the banner of Mosman FC. Happily, the team got off the ground and had a wonderful year. Mosman FC's president, Tess White, reports:

'It was a long, hard season with always not quite enough players—but they got to know each other—a major outcome. Got together socially at year's end—also major. The other teams in Manly Warringah loved them and often lent players to our team. Didn't win a game but scored some fine goals.

'Not having enough players also had a fabulously positive aspect—most of them had never played even half a game of sport in their lives, that is, during their entire school sporting careers. They had rather spent far too much time on benches, wishing. Due to the lack of players, they all played an entire game every week. Would finish shattered but gloriously included every week.

'This year they are back with a vengeance. A tremendous human being in all respects, and a fine football player approached us from another club, and he and three mates joined the ranks of the Mighty AL8Bs and we now have a fully-fledged team of 15 players for the 2009 season.'

Kevin's special place

Sometime, somewhere, someone has to send a strong bouquet to Parramatta Council for the job they have done on the Day of the Roses Memorial on the corner of Railway Parade and Carlton Street Granville, just over the road from where 83 Sydneysiders died in a train accident on 1977. In black granite, with the names of those killed engraved in white it is in the shade of beautiful trees, with lovely, well-cared-for shrubs all around and not the tiniest fleck of graffiti anywhere.

A local called Kevin comes there every day of his life, and has done since the day of the tragedy, when he spent 24 hours in the wreckage pulling the dead and injured out. For reasons he says he's not sure of, it just makes him feel peaceful, and he is apparently such a well-known figure in these parts that other locals refer to it as 'Kevin's summerhouse'.

Cauliflower hearts

Last Sunday, a couple of twin seven-year-old boys, Jude and Darcy, went with their 10-year-old sister, Audie, to their first rugby league game, the Tigers against the Warriors at Leichhardt Oval.* Sitting in the row behind them was a line of mature men of rugged visage and the odd bent nose, who made a series of pertinent comments about the play, the ref, etc.

It was only at half-time, when these gentlemen filed out of their seats and on to the oval, that the kids realised who they were—the surviving members of Balmain's mighty 1969 premiership-winning team. Those Tigers of '69 had been given special passes bearing their pictures, which they hung around their necks.

Midway through the second half, two of the wizened warriors leaned over with their passes and said: 'Would the boys like to have these?' As the beaming boys accepted, another of the Tigers greats detached his own, leant over and said: 'And one for the young girl.'

Gotta love this country! And good on you, Allan Fitzgibbon, Garry Leo and Bobby Smithies. We salute you.

*The Tigers were the Balmain Tigers until 1999 when they joined the Western Suburbs Magpies to become the West Tigers. Leichhardt Oval is the Balmain Tigers hallowed ground

How to celebrate

It was cold last Monday morning when criminal lawyer Andrew Tiedt was, with briefcase in hand and dressed for a day in court, walking along Castlereagh Street. Then he saw them. A large group of people, mostly males, spilling out of a pub, despite the early hour. Rowdy males.

Trouble? No. Soccer fans. Spanish ones! Cheering, waving flags, singing songs, the lot. Just a short time before, their team had won the World Cup for the first time and they were intent on continuing their wild celebrations.* Good-naturedly, they formed two lines and asked pedestrians to walk or run the gauntlet as they waved flags and sang.

On impulse, our man Tiedt decides to shout 'ESPANA!' as he runs between them. He doesn't make it. In an instant, the gauntlet closes in on him, picks him up, briefcase and all, and joyously throws him in the air six or seven times—Ole! Ole! OLE! OLE!—before letting him go on his way. Just another day in the life of an Australian city.

*Spain defeated the Netherland's 1-0 in extra time

Thumping tale of love in the fast lane

I heard the story last week of an Aussie bloke who worked out a novel way of asking his girlfriend a question that needed to be asked. Driving across the Anzac Bridge one evening with his arm out the window, he surreptitiously began thumping the door, even as he started to slow down, and gravely informed Sheila that he had a flat tyre.

Kneeling by the back left tyre as the traffic roared past, he called for her to open the glove-box, where she would find a small box and could she quickly bring it to him? Sheila did so and, at his request, opened it, while he remained kneeling by the tyre. There, sparkling back at her from the lights of the still-roaring traffic, was an engagement ring. What the? Will you marry me, Sheila? Yes, she would. They kissed, climbed back into the car, and drove off into the night.

There are a thousand stories in the steaming metropolis. This has been one of them.

Motherly throw-downs

Over the summer, up Wahroonga way, Phillip Ross was walking through the dappled light of his leafy suburb when he passed Comenarra Playing Fields and heard the unmistakable and timeless sound of leather on willow. And now, here they are!

In the nets, a young teenager in full cricket gear, with pads, gloves and helmet, is facing the worst his mother—in the lovely floral dress that is practically the female native uniform in those parts in January—can throw at him.

No, she is not bowling—she is hurling the balls at him from close range with one of those ball flickers you see at dog parks. And for safety's sake, mum is wearing a motorcycle helmet!

Road sage's jump-start for Swans

A couple of weeks ago, Vanlyn Davy was at the Swans–Geelong game at the SCG, and left early once it was obvious the Swannies were gone. How were they ever going to come back from a four-goal deficit? Besides, Van the Man had to get to Central Station for his long trip home, and it was good to get ahead of the crush. Still, as he ran across the park to the buses, a massive roar went up behind—the Swans had scored! And then another roar, bigger than the last!

It was a kind of weird feeling to be running in the darkness, away from the light and excitement, but the bus was ahead and he jumped on to get the last free seat . . . facing, as it turned out, a bus full of Swans supporters, all looking like someone had run over their dog—caught between anger and tears. Bloody Swannies. Let them down a-stinking-gain!

Still, aware of the positive noises he had heard before getting on the bus, our man Van turned his radio on and listened via the earpiece, the only man on the bus to be so in touch. The bus drones on, but our reader is getting more and more excited as the Swans close the gap, and the other travellers start to look at him quizzically. Grinding up a hill, with two seconds to go, the Swans score to hit the front!

Our reader jumps to his feet, no longer able to contain himself. 'GOOOOAAAAAAALLLLLL!!!!!!!,' yells he, and then again, 'GOOOOAAAAAALLLLLLLL!!!!'

The bus of stunned mullets stare back, unmoved. Our reader can't figure it. Why aren't they with him in his excitement?

Then Van twigs. He is not dressed like them. To the Swans supporters he looks like a supremely provocative Cats fan, making their miserable lives even more unbearable.

So he repeats it once more, 'GOOOAAAAALLLLLL!' . . . but this time adds, 'SWWWAAAAAANNNSSS!!!!!!' As one, the bus goes berserk, the more so when they realise that Jesus lives, that the hour of their redemption is now, that there has been a miracle in Sydney town, and the Swans have WON!

The bus lurches now as people stand on their feet, roar the Swans' victory song, throw their tickets and programs in the air, and explode with joy. Long have they suffered, but now is dinkum their hour.

'When we got to Central,' the reader writes, 'a lot of them treated me as a hero, as if I had scored the winning goal myself. I quietly explained to them that I was particularly happy that night because my first love, the Balmain Tigers, had also had a big win that night over at the Olympic stadium. Wow!! What a night out in Sydney town!!' Gotta love this country!

I love Sydney because . . .

- You can make more than $100,000 per year and still can't afford a house.
- You never bother looking at the train timetable because you know the drivers have never seen it either.
- You spend 30 minutes in a traffic jam next to a car that has more power going to its speakers than its wheels.
- Your taxi driver was a microsurgeon before he migrated to Australia.
- You've been to more than one baby shower that has two mothers and a sperm donor.
- A man in full leather regalia and crotchless chaps gets on the bus and you don't notice.
- Your hairdresser is straight, your plumber is gay, and your Avon lady is a drag queen.

Our lives at the beach are in safe hands

Last weekend a hundred odd 12-year-old and 13-year-old junior lifesavers attended the Sydney branch surf lifesaving development camp. These kids are the best of the best in surf lifesaving, representing their clubs from North Bondi to Burning Palms.

The gathering involved two full days of fun and serious instruction, before Sunday afternoon's Club Rescue and Resuscitation Championship between the top 20 clubs—effectively the last time the boys and girls can compete on roughly equal footing before the puberty power game takes over. The five Clovelly girls, together since the under-6s, are a formidable team, thus leaving two Clovelly lads to seek a composite team. But hang on, what's that over there? Three tall, bronzed, athletic North Cronulla girls ... Umm, would they be interested in forming a team with two skinny lads from the east? Absolutely, no problems!

The heats start. Tim and Fearghus are the swim rescue members, Daisy and Taylor are the resuscitation specialists and the unflappable Renee is the team captain. Iconic club teams start falling away, a semi-final place is suddenly in the offing, and coach Dave fires up as they sweat and strain their way to win after win. 'We can have a real crack at this!'

They make the semis! And it's against the Clovelly girls! As they hit the water, and pound the beach and the chests of the dummies to bring them back to life, chief judge Doug is all over them like an XL rashie on a 6-year-old nipper. His face shows the anguish of competition—just a few grains of procedural sand separate the teams but, alas, a small slip sees both teams eliminated from the final . . .

So, who finally won?

We did.

Swim easy Sydney, our lives at the beach this summer, and for many years to come, are in great hands. Bravo, you junior lifesavers, and the volunteers who shape them.

Another late leaver

Recent NSW Premier Morris Iemma lived at home with his parents until the age of 35. He then rose to great prominence, not as someone who likes to do strange things with chickens or the like, but as a happily married and very successful politician. When I mentioned this fact in my column, I pondered, lonely as a cloud, whether in the modern age there was anyone else in the country who could make a similar claim.

Very quickly, the answer came back: John Winston Howard! The Prime Minister lived with his mum till he was 32, before marrying Janette and moving out.

Memo Glenn: just leave the sledging to us

One of our informants attended the England v NSW cricket match last Sunday at the SCG and, prior to play, wandered around to the nets and noticed England's Paul Collingwood batting against a bowling machine. As he watched, the first ball came down . . . to be confidently clipped through the mid-wicket area.

All well and good, but another Sydneysider who was watching couldn't help himself. 'McGrath doesn't bowl there,' he told the Englishman firmly.

Collingwood ignored him and simply greeted the next ball with another crashing blade, to send it hurtling through the cover area . . . only to receive a comment from the same man: 'McGrath doesn't bowl there, either.'

The third ball, pitched just outside off stump, moved a touch off the seam and took the edge of the Englishman's bat, flying to precisely the spot where a slip would have taken a comfortable catch.

'That's where McGrath bowls!' said our man. Ah, if looks could kill.

Tartan-ic effort

Last Sunday in the under-10 finals, the Lindfield Tartans were due to play the Mosman Whales. Beforehand, the Tartans' tighthead prop, Dan, came down with a bug, and his mum Donna sent out a group email asking the team for any quick-fix remedies they might have. Team manager Russell was soon in with his reply:

'Donna, to start with, try him on the lemon juice, and make sure he has lots of sleep and rest and give him plenty of drugs. Then on Saturday night, show him the Souths v Manly grand final in 1970 (when Satts broke his jaw) . . . some tapes of Tommy Raudonikis . . . John Donnelly and Les Boyd . . . Steve Finnane whispering in Graham Price's ear in the Test against Wales at the SCG in 1978 . . . and then bring out the DVD of the '91 and the '99 World Cups and stand in your living room and sing the national anthem.

'Then take him out the back and tell him to look up into the sky. Say to him, "Daniel, 50 years from now, when you look back on your life and regret all the things you could have done and all things you could have been, make sure one of them isn't that you didn't get a chance when you were 10 to stick it to those Mosman kids with their Wallaby dads and their gym junkie mothers. Don't leave it on the table son; you might only get one shot at the title."

'Then remind him that the reason God made him in the image of a bookend is because there can be no greater calling in life and no greater honour than to pack down in the engine room of the game they play in heaven and to lead those pigs forward into battle and into history. Apply a bit of Dencorub to his chest and send him to bed with plenty of encouragement and a hot water bottle.'

Daniel played, and the Tartans won, as John Eales and Phil Kearns—and their *charming* wives, thank you very much—looked on stoically.

Morning, guv'nor

Just another sleepy Sunday afternoon in Sydney, down on the peninsula. At the Gloria Jean's coffee shop in Narrabeen, there are perhaps a dozen people at the tables when in walks a casually dressed but distinguished looking lady who orders a coffee. After a brief chat with the owner, who recognises her, the lady sits down and proceeds to drink her coffee and read the newspaper.

None of the other people in the coffee shop take any particular note and, after 20 minutes, she gets up, says goodbye to the staff and is gone—likely to a reception at Government House. For it was our most respected Governor of NSW, Her Excellency Marie Bashir.

Mettle detected

A while back, when heading through the metal detectors at the Ansett terminal . . . come to think of it, make that a looong while back . . . I fondly remember noting that the bloke ahead of me being frisked was the then deputy prime minister, Tim Fischer. Now Mr Fischer was an unlikely man to be carrying a gun, even if he was the leader of the National Party at the time, but what was most impressive was that there was not the slightest hint of complaint from him.

Against that, however, Gough Whitlam mentioned to me this week that when he and his beloved wife of the past 62 years, Margaret, had been heading to Cairns last month from Sydney, Mrs Whitlam had set off the alarm. When she had informed the security guard that it was her pacemaker, the guard had replied 'show me the scar', which she did.

Oddly enough, I do not take this as a great and enduring sign of Australian egalitarianism so much as the sign of an INSOLENT YOUNG PUNK WHO SHOULD BE TAKEN OUT AND HORSEWHIPPED!

Third drop

Last week I lightly chipped Australian batsman Ed Cowan for referring to himself in the third person in this quote: 'There is nothing to say Phil Hughes and Ed Cowan can't play in the same Test team, whether that's opening or middle order.'

In reply, Ed dropped me a note on Monday:

Dear Peter,

Many moons ago while playing for Syd Uni CC at Uni number one, I made a bet with my best friend, that I could weasel my way into 'The Fitz Files' through either an indiscriminate reference to myself in the third person or by using a ridiculous mixed metaphor. I am a little disappointed to be honest that it has taken this long— there were at least two instances last season that I thought I was a certainty. When we cross paths next, be sure to hit me up for a beer. I am now 10 heavier in the wallet. Keep entertaining.

Best,

Ed Cowan

Got me!

Three cheers

Last Saturday afternoon Joeys First XV were about to take on their Oakhill College counterparts in a trial. All is ready for the traditional beginning, as more than 1000 Joeys lads, in their blue blazers and shiny shoes, form up a tunnel and begin singing at the top of their voices: 'YOU'LL NEVER WALK . . . ALONE!' even as the First XV in their cerise and blue jerseys file on to the field.

Strangely, however, this time the school chums don't disperse, but instead keep the chant going over and over again as, slowly, carefully, the bobbing heads of the Oakhill First XV are seen just above the throng as they make their own way through the same tunnel. 'YOU'LL NEVER WALK . . . ALONE!'

What is going on? Oh. Oh, I see. Look there. The Oakhill lads are being led out by the cousin of one of them, a critically ill lad in a wheelchair—Jack is a 10-year-old with an inoperable brain tumour, who will never have the privilege to walk himself through such a tunnel of honour. And still the lads keep going . . . The young man smiles, acknowledges the chant from a school which is not his, and it keeps going for all of two minutes, as both teams make their way to the middle, still led by Jack, and when they get there the entire gathering offers him a mighty three cheers.

Now the Joeys captain comes to shake his hand, and then introduces his team, one by one, as the crowd keeps cheering, right up to the point when he comes off the field and the game begins.

Streaker protocol

A disturbing report has come to hand from Griffith's Parramatta vs Penrith trial last Saturday evening. Sadly, the people of Griffith appear to have let themselves down badly.

Unscheduled half-time 'entertainment' consisted of a real live streaker hopping the fence near the clubhouse and bolting straight across the halfway line, and over the fence on the other side. Extraordinarily, our naked Flash Gordon carried his own clothes and shoes throughout his mad dash. First point, for you Griffos: Whoever heard of streakers having to carry their own clothes? Are we to believe that the poor bastard didn't have one friend to keep his gear for him? Shame on you!

And then, when the streaker got to the other side, of course the local constabulary did whatever the equivalent of 'collaring' is when the person they're grabbing doesn't actually have a collar to collar. As the police, ahem, apprehended the said Caucasian male proceeding in a westerly direction, the spectators nearby gathered round to laugh. Yes, *laugh*. Which brings us to the most serious black mark against the Griffos. Listen, you lot, the correct Australian form (refer *Official Australian Streakers Protocol & Etiquette Manual*, 1978, Starkus, John and Newdie, Roody) when police grab a streaker at a sporting event is to engage in some good-hearted booing.

The police then must put on their grim faces, like they're just doing their job, Sir, Ma'am, while being secretly thrilled that they actually have something to do. But whatever else, we spectators *don't* laugh when the streaker gets nabbed, got it? It is un-Australian. Don't let it happen again.

Point of order

On Wednesday afternoon at Federal Parliament, the Government and the Opposition were going at it hammer and tongs, macho and mincing, when the Speaker of the House, Harry Jenkins, noticed an esteemed visitor in the public gallery. Of course, he did what he had to do. He stopped proceedings—ordah! . . . ORDAH!—so as to extend a formal welcome.

'I cannot believe that I am about to do this as a Fitzroy and Brisbane Lions supporter,' he said, 'but I inform the house that we have present in the gallery this afternoon Ronald Dale Barassi, a great Australian Rules footballer.'

Applause all round, to which Barassi responded with gracious nods of the head. But a point of order, if I may, Mr Speaker. Surely the correct terminology would be to welcome Barassi as '*the* great Australian Rules footballer'? Still, good on you.

LIVER-CAUGHT CORNEA-BOWLED KIDNEY

Nice touch

I am told that at the end of each match they play, members of the Australian Transplant Cricket team huddle on the ground and give thanks to the 22 players on their team—the 11 who took the field for their second innings in life, and for the other 11 who made it possible through a transplant of organ donation and the gift of life. Lovely.

Watch warms old digger's heart

Back in the early days of the Second World War, two teenagers, Joe Dawson and Elaine Colbran, sat holding hands in the front parlour of her parents' house in Melbourne. Joe was about to leave for New Guinea where he would be right in the thick of the fighting on the Kokoda Track, but before he went Elaine gave him three precious things that she'd been saving up for months to buy: rosary beads, a small leather case with images of six saints in them to keep him safe, and a silver wrist watch with a personal inscription from her on the back. Joe treasured all three, but in his first major action in New Guinea a bomb landed close enough that the watch was torn from his wrist and to his bitter regret he never saw it again.

I mentioned this episode in passing in my book on Kokoda and, during the week, Joe got a phone call at his home in Forster, on the NSW Mid North Coast. It was from another digger who'd fought there, Bill Franks. He'd read the yarn in the book and it reminded him of a watch he'd picked up in the jungle 60-odd years ago, which he still had.

A few days later, a package arrived in Forster. Elaine and Joe now married for 62 years opened it. Elaine took one look and burst into tears. It was the watch.

Little rays of sunshine

The mighty Asquith Magpies under-6 rugby league side—composed of four- to six-year-olds—has been doing it tough in recent weeks with all the wet weather having caused game after game to be cancelled. The littlies from the Pennant Hills Stags under-6s were feeling the same, which is why there was relief all round when the game between the two sides took place last week—even though the Magpies had to borrow a Stag, because they were missing a player.

These are the kind of games where numbers on the field are restricted to seven a side, and most players aren't aware of what the score is at any given moment. The difference here was that, because it had been such a break, the Stags reserves were *desperate* to get on too. So, with five minutes to go, the question was asked. Could the Pennant Hills Stags reserves come on, too? No problem from the ref, or the Magpies, or the Asquith parents.

The Pennant Hills Stags' under-6 match report tells what happened next: '. . . In the final five minutes the whole team ended up on the field with kindly no objection from the Asquith side. Asquith still managed to score despite a defence of 11, but what did it matter when we saw the smiles on all the kids' faces, who were just happy to be finally playing a game of their beloved footy after two weeks of patiently waiting for the fields to dry . . .'

Victory at last

Ain't life grand? Last year, the Pacific Hills Dural Pumas under-17 women's soccer team was formed from a group of school friends who not only had never played together before, but for the most part had never played before, full stop. Not surprisingly, they went through the 2009 season without a victory.

This year, with the team reduced to just 11 players because of Year 11 study commitments, they were beaten in every game, conceding over 100 goals, the highest score being a 26-0 reverse in which, as the saying goes, they were lucky to get to nil. Despite not scoring a goal all year, all 11 fronted up to training and games week after week. Last Sunday, however, they played a valiant Macquarie Dragons team and an amazing thing happened. In the first half, not only did they score a goal, but the Dragons didn't! Could they hold on?

Tension rises around the ground as history beckons. With 10 minutes to go, the ball goes to the Dragons striker, who belts it hard. The Pumas goalkeeper flies forward and to her right, reaches out and . . . blocks it! Not long after, the final whistle blows and, after one year, four months and 90 minutes of a hard-fought tussle, the Pumas have victory. As tears, cheers and pandemonium breaks out, the girls are swamped by fans and congratulated by the Dragons.

Humour at work

Over the past few years and, in some cases still now, a committed Ms Sydneysider could have bought something special from her favourite lingerie shop in Dural called Breast Dressed, before having her hair done at the hairdresser known as Lillie Pilli of Kirribilli, and then snacking at the Chatswood sandwich shop The Upper Crust. Mr Sydney, meanwhile, could have done business with the Surry Hills brokers known as Legal Eagal, Beagal and Briefcase before dropping into the Better Read Than Dead bookstore in Newtown, then meeting friends for lunch at the Italian sandwich joint in Bondi known as—drum roll, if you please, maestro—HowtheFoccacia.

Together, they could have their driveway re-laid by William the Concretor (he came, he saw, he concreted) and, on a trip north to Byron, be amused to see a household rubbish removalist called Getta Garbo and a septic tank drainer called Mr Whiffy.

Other genuine Sydney businesses include: Femme For Tile (Tile and Bathroom Accessories); HolySheet! (Homewares); The Lone Drainer (Plumbing); What A Load of Rubbish (Garbage); Drop Your Pants (Dry Cleaner) and Viagra Scaffolding—We'll Get It Up For You.

Last, but not . . .

Last week, during the NSW Life Saving Championships at Kingscliff, two 12 year-old girls were competing in the distance swim section. One girl was coming a creditable second last, well in front of the last place getter. However, the girl coming last asked her to slow down and stay with her because she was scared on her own and especially scared of sharks. So she slowed and both girls swam in together in last place, and upon landing on the beach hugged warmly.

Slammin' Sam

Last Saturday, Shore 16Cs, playing Newington 16Bs, managed a meagre 46 runs in a 30-over game. In reply, Newington were 5–44 with 10 overs to spare and it was obviously all over. Step up Sam Roberts, to bowl for Shore.

Can you see it coming? The Newington lads barely did. First ball, no run. Second ball, wicket! Third ball, wicket! Fourth ball, no run. Fifth ball, wicket! Sixth ball wicket! And 9–44 at the end of the over! Sensational stuff . . . Richie? Well, Richie Benaud wasn't there, but he should have been.

In the next over, Newington made two runs to level the scores and the ball was tossed back to Sam—on a hat-trick, with the game in the balance. He runs in. It loops, it lands, it hisses, it knocks off the bail! Got 'im!

The draw is secured. Handshakes all round. The Newington boys took it well. And 22 lads have some wonderful material for school reunions, 50 years hence.

On a roll

Back in October 2008, the Marrickville Bowling Club was—like nigh on every other bowling club in the land—seriously struggling. Memberships were down, interest was waning, and Penury the next stop after Penshurst. And that was when local resident Peter Manson and a friend decided to establish a gay lawn bowls group, playing out of the club. Neither had ever played but what the hey? They decided to call themselves 'Unbiased' and started to learn.

Two-and-half years on they have approximately 40 members whose major activity is playing every Sunday at 1pm. A fortnight ago, 18 Unbiased members attended the Asia-Pacific Outgames in Wellington and came back after winning 18 medals, and they are also playing in the current pennant season. By the way, the club is not restricted to gays only.

Tri-er honoured

Imagine the scene. While the rest of Sydney sat in gridlocked traffic on Sunday morning, 1500 triathletes were running, riding and swimming from first light. Of course, once one has finished such an event, the general thing is to burst through the finish line before collapsing to the ground as you allow the blessed feeling of achievement to wash over you. Then the form is to stagger back to the 'transition zone' to retrieve your bike. But there is a strict protocol involved: it is considered very poor form to get that bike until the last competitor has completed the cycle course.

So it was that on Sunday morning, a hundred or so of the first finishers, all of them as lean as greyhounds, wander over to find that although it is more than two hours since they had gone through this section, they still can't get on their bikes and go home, because there are still competitors who haven't gone through yet. So they wait, some more patiently than others.

Finally though, a good 10 minutes after the penultimate competitor, the last man arrives. He's hurting, but he's still going. A large bull of a man of oriental appearance, he either dismounts or falls off his carbon-fibre steed—it's hard to tell—and jogs very, very slowly, with his bike towards the transition.

Many hundreds of eyes watch on in a curious silence until suddenly, in a beautiful moment, the swollen crowd rises in unison to clap and cheer with genuine warmth, encouragement and appreciation for the efforts of a fellow competitor who is struggling, but still game. The big man remains a study of exhausted, single-minded focus, but now continues with a slight spring in his step.

Run, Sam, run

Last weekend at Booralee Oval in Botany, the Eastern Suburbs Cricket Club's under-13 side was caught two players short going up against the mighty South Sydney Mount Carmel Juniors side, and were obliged to call on a couple of younger brothers to fill in. One, Tom Linnstrom, normally plays under-11s, while the other, Sam Kertesz, is an under-9s player.

The game begins. Tom ably keeps wickets for half the innings, while young Sam, in his boardshorts and T-shirt, helps out in the field. Hopefully, hidden at the bottom of the line-up, the two young 'uns won't need to bat. But, of course, as cricket is wont to do, things don't turn out like that and they really are needed.

Tom, batting at number 10, does himself proud and scores just enough to get the team to the point where the scores are tied, before he slightly misjudges a clever ball and is caught behind. All eyes now turn to the small figure nervously making his way out to the crease, trailing a bat that almost looks too big for him to carry. There has, in fact, been a small delay, as everyone has scrambled to find pads, helmet and bat small enough for him in an under-13s kit bag.

The eight-year-old Sam takes strike and the 12-year-old fast bowler roars in. The first ball hits Sam high in the thigh, too high for an lbw, but it renders a stinging blow nevertheless. Brushing away the tears that are welling up, so he can see the next ball, Sam readies himself.

It zips off the wicket, rising fast, but Sam is now experienced in this game and swings. He connects! The ball goes straight over the worthy bowler's head and, to the chants of 'Run, Sam, RUN!', he takes off like a scalded cat. The instant his bat crosses the far crease to secure the winning run, his teammates rush on to the field, led by his older brother, Zac, and, after engulfing him with congratulations, they chair him from the field.

The good sports that make the South Sydney Mount Carmel side come to him afterwards, shake his hand and tell him 'Well played', 'You were too good for us', 'Good hit', which Sam modestly accepts. Kids' sport as it should be.

Last bus home

At 10pm last Sunday, two completely exhausted bushwalkers training for the 100 kilometre Oxfam walk, staggered out of the bush at Seaforth Oval after just managing to complete a 34km section of the walk. Alas, no taxi company was interested in coming to pick them up, as they could not provide a 'house number', so they had no choice but to start to gingerly limp home. It was cold, lonely and hobbling horrible.

But wait, what's that? An engine. After 20 minutes, the first vehicle to come past them proved to be a bus, which they furiously hailed. True, it was going the other way to where they were heading, but no worries, mateys, after hearing their story the driver told them he'd take them to Manly, so they could get a cab. But, hey, bugger it. When they got to Manly the driver told them he'd changed his mind and, after putting 'Dee Why Special' up on his destination board, drove them all the way home.

He was a cricket tragic to the end.

Ashes to ashes

A couple were over for dinner last Saturday evening, and the woman mentioned to the host that the next day, they were going to pick up her father's ashes as he recently passed away. When he asked her where they were going to be placed, she offered: 'I will see if the Australian Cricket Board is interested, they don't have *any* ashes at the moment.'*

*England won the 2009 Ashes series 2-1

Go, David, go

David Hurwitz, known to his many friends as 'DH7', is a fine young man with a mild intellectual disability. The 15-year-old has a passion for soccer and, as his older brother, Danny, is coach of the under-11s and under-12s Ku-ring-gai representative soccer teams, he has been a constant presence at their trainings and games as their number 1 supporter, key motivational speaker and main helper-outerer.

For the past few months the running gag between David and the team has been for them to ask if he scored a goal in his own game for Lindfield FC under-16s the day before, and for him to reply, 'I nearly scored . . . but missed by this much', holding up his fingers a couple of centimetres apart. High hilarity all round. Those same kids, however, decided that it would be good to go and cheer for David too.

So, last Saturday, 20 of them, plus their parents plus 15 first-graders from Lindfield FC, showed up to support David in his game against Asquith at Lindfield UTS. With such a cheer squad, David played his heart out even more than usual, as every touch raised a roar. No mucking around, it was a tense game, with the score locked at 2-2 in the second half as the minutes ebbed away. But wait, the ball is coming his way . . .!

A centre kick from Lindfield. A deflection back to David! Calm and quick, he draws his right foot back and then . . . strikes like a cobra! GOAL! The cheers were heard in neighbouring suburbs.

Sporting gesture

Here's one for all those teams that strove valiantly this season—playing for love alone—only to just miss out when the laurels were being handed out. It comes from a letter penned by Ben Chiarella, the Sydney Uni Hockey Club third grade coach and club captain, after his team was just pipped in overtime of the grand final by a valiant Manly side: 'I'm sure we all dream of winning a premiership, however the dreams we don't see is what occurred in our change room before the game with a united group of friends about to do battle, singing the team song, the team coming together 25 weeks ago as relative strangers and finishing as best of mates. You may read this thinking "Who cares, you didn't win the grand final . . ." You are right, we didn't win the grand final, but I and the 13 members of Sunday's losing team have this funny feeling that we actually won this season.'

The perfect medicine

I am reliably informed that the following is not an urban myth, but dinkum happened in a certain aged-care facility recently.

A circular went out to say that no one was allowed to drink tap water unless it was boiled, and there was to be no more rock-melon or strawberries as they have pitted skins and there could be dangerous microbes in the pores.

Needless to say, many of the old folk were far from impressed, with one sweet little old lady just on 90 years old snorting, quick as a flash: 'Next, they will be telling us we can't have sex.'

On the ball

At a function in Perth last week, yours truly did a little light pal-ing around with Adam Gilchrist, Mark Bosnich and Dermott Brereton, and a couple of the stories that emerged bear repeating.

The first is a tip for young soccer goalies from Bosnich, who played for Manchester United and the Socceroos among others, and is of course among the greatest goalkeepers this country has ever produced. When I asked him what would be going through his head in the goal square when an opponent was lining up the ball just 11 metres away—as in when there was a penalty shoot-out—he replied immediately. 'I always just concentrated on the non-striking foot. When a right-footed bloke was lining up the kick, nine times of 10 his left foot was pointing to where the ball was going to go, and as soon as he struck it I would hurl myself in that direction.' Brilliant, isn't it?

As for Brereton, I was interested to hear that back in the mid-1950s his late father sat on the bench for the Irish rugby team. 'I once asked him,' the Hawthorn legend recounted, 'what he had done so well that year to get so close to the Test team. "Did you score a lot of tries, Dad?" "None at all, son," he replied. "Did you kick a lot of goals, then?" "No son, not one, I was a forward." "Pull off some great tackles, at least?" "Not particularly, son." "Well, what did you do so well, Dad?" "Well, that year I seem to mostly remember a lot of great pushing in the scrum!"'

A bloke outrage

'We are Australian'.

This morning, I shall don my traditional Australian costume, and engage in a traditional Australian pastime—after searching the bottom of the laundry basket and sorting through the crap in the back of my car, I will finally locate and put on my scungy old footie shorts, my odd socks, and my T-shirt with paint stains, before going to have a game of touch football. On my way, I'll pass similarly attired blokes, going for a run or a game of park tennis. It's what we Australian blokes do. At least most of us do. There is a notable exception, however.

I am talking about you uppity cyclists. What the hell is it with you show-ponies? Why, when we are dressed in scunge and grunge, just like our fathers taught us, and their fathers taught them, do each and every one of you look like you're trying out for the Tour de France fashion show?

Every weekend! There you are, in ludicrously tight Lycra outfits covered in the same logos that your heroes have sold their souls for, 'cept yours don't quite hold in your flabby thighs and tubby tummies. You set it all off with designer dark glasses and designer shoes—and I have the distinct impression that your entire outfits can be found in the one drawer at home, all neatly pressed and freshly washed, probably by a man-servant called Julio.

And then you sit around in cafes for hours afterwards, looking like billboards for everything un-Australian. What the RUCK is going on with you people?

I COULD BE SO LUCKY

How's your form?

Australian Government Department of Immigration and Multicultural and Indigenous Affairs Application for Grant of Australian Citizenship Test.

1. How many slabs can you fit in the back of a Falcon ute while also allowing room for your cattle dog?

2. Name three of the Daddo brothers.

3. Would you eat pineapple on pizza? Would you eat egg on a pizza?

4. Who are Scott and Charlene?

5. How do you apply your tomato sauce to a pie? a) Squirt and spread with finger. b) Sauce injection straight into the middle.

6. Which Australian prime minister held the world record for drinking a yardie full of beer the fastest?

7. What is someone more likely to die of:
   a) Red-back spider.
   b) Great white shark.
   c) Victorian police officer.
   d) King brown snake.
   e) Your missus after a big night.
   f) Dropbear.

Save the best for last

Last Saturday young Harry Werner was playing with the Cromer under-13 cricket team he has just joined against Wakehurst. Cromer was bowling.

Harry was given the ball in the last over, and his first ball was hit to mid-off and caught—a no-ball, so no wicket. The next few balls got belted, but no worries. Ben, the astute captain of the side, brought the field in close. On Harry's last ball, a pearler, the batsman edged behind to the keeper, who took a great catch. A WICKET!

Harry went mad, his team went mad, his father went mad. Wakehurst took it all with grace and good sportsmanship. What a great game cricket is. Harry has autism.

Iron boys

You have to picture the scene. Last Sunday morning, the local nippers were competing in the ocean swim and beach run. The furious battle was particularly hard fought as the pack moved forward through the water and over the sand, until the closing stage when two young blokes made their move and surged out in front.

Both were about 10 years old, though while one tall and lithe with a long leg stride, the other smaller and lighter, skimming over the sand rather than pounding forward. The crowd cheered, the Pacific Ocean roared its approval even as the waves themselves charged in to get a better look, and the boys powered towards the sole flag. The big lad . . .? No . . . the smaller lad might be just in front. Even as the crowd continued to cheer, the two boys magically grew into ironmen, until finally, neck-and-neck, the smaller one just managed to pip him at the post. Victory!

And yet, although their lungs are on fire and they are both gasping for air, the young winner actually does have an ounce of energy left, which he now uses to grip the bigger lad's hand who . . . grips the proffered hand in reply, and topples over, exhausted, as all the other nippers crowd around congratulating them both.

The whole lot of them were last seen all building sandcastles while their proud parents gorged on the sausage sizzle. Gotta love this country!

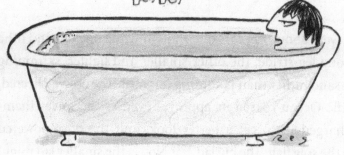

The water calls,
I feel its tug.
Best to the depths
and pull the plug.

Salty verses

While competing in the Cole Classic marathon swim on Sunday, Fitzphile Jim Thompson found himself swimming by a one-legged bloke and composed the following poem in his head, called 'The Ocean Swimmer':

I'm lifted by the sea's cool hands,
The crowds are cheering from the sands,
I don't perform amazing feats,
My victory is that I compete.

What an over

Last Saturday at Forsyth Park in Neutral Bay, the unbeaten Loreto Kirribilli cricket team played local rivals Wenona. Loreto, who won the toss and elected to bat, scored 84 runs in their allotted 12-over innings. As the temperature reached about 35 degrees, the first Wenona pair scored 27 and Loreto were on the back foot. The ball was then thrown to Julia Baker, a year 5 student.

Although the first bowl of her over was a wide, the next delivery was a dot ball. And then Julia unleashed a pearler, resulting in the fielder at short leg taking a lovely clean catch. Her next ball was even better, as she sent the stumps flying. Young Julia was on a hat-trick, and the excited spectators hovered close . . . when the ball was hit to square leg and another beautiful catch was taken. The crowd cheered, teammates congratulated her.

Still there were two balls to go, though, and on the fifth ball of the over, Julia again sent the stumps flying. More cheers, more congratulations. And then to the final ball of the over—a carbon copy of the preceding delivery, once again taking out the stumps.

Five wickets from five consecutive deliveries. Needless to say, Loreto won, while Wenona was gracious in defeat and generous in praise. Smiles and congratulations all round and not a trophy in sight—it was cricket at its best, played in the game's true spirit.

Superhuman effort

Last Sunday was one of those perfect wintry sunny days. At a soccer field in Sydney's west, the Winston Hills under-18 girls' soccer team, coming last in the comp—with 39 goals scored against them, and only five goals on their side of the ledger—turn up to find that, due to school holidays, they have only seven players. Their opponents, the Castle Hill Rockets, positioned third in the comp, will be coming for them. And yet, honour must be served.

Before kick-off, the Winston Hill girls gather in the centre and avow that they will do their all to keep the Rockets down to less than 10 goals. To the few parents sitting on the hill, the young women look lonely and forlorn standing out in the centre as the full-strength Rockets, looking professional, jog out single file to shake hands.

Fifteen minutes in, though, the score is still nil-all. Thirty minutes in ... *still* nil-all! What's happening? The girls are playing the best they have all season, defending, intercepting passes and even pushing upfield against the odds to create chances and shoot for goal. They're playing like maniacs! Half-time ... still nil-all! The girls collapse on the sideline and their hovering parents, though delighted, expect a second-half slaughter as crippling exhaustion sets in.

And yet, though indeed exhausted, their daughters' crazy dream begins to grow—and with 10 minutes to go, they have still held their valiant opponents to nil! The few supporters try to keep the girls going, praying that the whistle will blow. Please hang on. The keeper calls out encouragement to the six girls trying to cover the whole field. At last, the full-time whistle peals around the field!

Never before has nil–all been so celebrated. The Winston Hills girl either jump with elation or collapse on the ground as their gracious opponents offer three hearty cheers of congratulations, as does the referee in quieter fashion.

Go Toonies!

Back in 1979, a group of 15- to 16-year-old boys from Marist Brothers Parramatta held a cricket match at the start of their Christmas holidays. The boys in the group, who hailed from the Toongabbie–Girraween area, had challenged all other comers . . . and the first Toony Locals v the Rest of the World game was the result.

Every year since, on the last Sunday before Christmas—and it has not rained *once* in that time—the 'boys' get back together for the annual clash. Tomorrow marks the 33rd year—same mates, same ground, same rules. (Although it should be noted that Rule B, which states 'no girls', and used to be very unpopular with the girlfriends, is extremely popular with their now wives.) The score stands at 16 wins each, with tomorrow offering boasting rights of dominance.

Mudbath time

You have to imagine the scene. Last weekend, the grand finals for Nepean District Soccer were held at Jamison Park, Penrith. The Penrith FC under-10s side had won every game through the season, and was taking on the second-placed Blaxland boys in the first game of Saturday morning, unperturbed by the field being a sea of mud after an overnight deluge.

After a battle worthy of these two teams of tiny titans, the scores were level at 1–1 with seconds to go when a Penrith striker managed to roar home a ripper of a goal with the last kick of the game. In a great show of sportsmanship the two sides shook hands, cheered each other and then, as one mixed group, went and applauded the mums, dads and supporters on each side of the field.

Then all of a sudden they took off. Running towards the mud pit that was the goal square at the northern end, upon reaching it they dived head-first into the mud and rolled around in it, emerging only when a panicked voice on the PA told them to stop.

To cap it off, during the presentation ceremony, the MC asked who was going to wash the jumpers, to which the only girl among the two teams quickly replied: 'My dad'.

Small delights of political retirement

The best speech of the week goes to Bob Hawke who, reportedly, addressed the good and the great at the Hordern Pavilion on Monday night, in his capacity as chairman of Bestest, whatever that is.

Surely the most charismatic man to have held our nation's highest office, he noted it was nice to (a) be at a function where you aren't up to your arse in coleslaw, and (b) work with an organisation where your number 2 isn't trying to shaft you.

It's catching

Here is an excerpt from the report of the coach of the Randwick Thunder under-12 cricket team, after they played Easts Dynamite last weekend:

'One final mention of an incident I witnessed today that truly epitomised what I like to see in our boys. Chris Roach, after being dismissed by a wonderful catch at gully, Chris went straight up to his opponent and shook his hand and said: "Great catch mate". As much as everyone, none more than myself, want to win games, things like this represent what kids' sport and in fact all sport is about—and that is respect. Well done Roachy— you did yourself and our team proud today.'

Fans past it

It is the second day of the Sydney Test, Australia is being completely hammered, and my informant is seated ten rows in front of the Barmy Army. After they had just finished a chant about 'You all live in a convict colony', the two guys behind him have this exchange.

'Mate, why do you reckon these Poms insist on living in the past?'

'Mate, if you were a Pom, wouldn't you want to live in the past?'

A Super salute

The scene was set at Balgowlah RSL last Saturday evening, with 300 people crowding in to watch the Super 14 final between the Waratahs and Crusaders on the big screens. Twenty minutes in, the crowd is well oiled, gesturing and shouting at several screens. Over in Christchurch, Phil Waugh and his fellow Tahs were responding, playing out of their collective tree. When Waratahs winger Lachie Turner leapt high over Dan Carter to score the first try, the place exploded. Tears, cheers, more beers! But settle, Petal, here they go again.

At exactly 5.59pm, the Tahs launch yet another attack, when suddenly the sound is muted, as a voice asks everyone to turn to the west and observe a minute's silence for fallen Diggers. As one, everyone stands and turns to the west, and is genuinely silent, even though they continue watching . . .

Lachie Turner! He's doing a chip and chase! He's got it on the toe! He's re-gathered! He's racing for the line! He's SCORED!

Still not a peep, not a murmur. Just an electric current of excitement going through the whole room. But the Diggers must come first. On the field, the Waratahs are wild in their celebrations. At the Balgowlah RSL, the mixed crowd of Australians and Kiwis, heirs to the Anzacs, remain totally silent.

At last, however, the words come to signal the minute's silence is over: 'Lest . . . we . . . forget.' Then, and only then, does the room explode once more with deafening roars.

Up periscope!

Poms living on past glories reminds David Apostolidis of an episode during the 2006 World Cup where, on the evening after Australia recorded their fabulous 2–2 draw against Croatia, some Pommy fans started singing to a thousand Australians, to the tune of 'Yellow Submarine': 'You all live in a convict colony'.

In full voice, the Australian battalion roared back, to the same tune, and in unison: 'You sent us to a sunny paradise . . . a sunny paradise . . . a sunny paradise!' To their eternal credits, the Poms applauded and kept on walking.

Pitching in

On a Sunday morning in January, in a NSW Major League baseball game between Manly and Blacktown at Frenchs Forest, the Manly team was rather bemused to see the veteran opposition starting pitcher suddenly call time during the first inning, step back off the mound and have a discreet vomit. No doubt a fierce hangover was biting back, what?

Still, it was surprising. This was a fierce match: First v. third on the table, and there was bad blood between the teams. The last time the two had faced each other there had been a benches-clearing brawl, after which three players were ejected. And now the pitcher had been so heavily on the sauce the night before that he was vomiting? It didn't fit.

No, it didn't. And then they found out. It wasn't grog: the pitcher was in fact in the middle of a round of chemo and radio-therapy. Manly went on to win the match, played in good spirit this time, with all the Manly players certain to shake the pitcher's hand and honour him for his courage. In reply, the pitcher could barely speak above a hoarse whisper, but appreciated their good wishes. Neville Peters of the Blacktown Workers baseball team, the Manly team salutes you. As do we.

Hats off to some fantastic Indian fans

Last Sunday at the SCG in the ODI between Australia and India, two large Sikh men suddenly whipped the hats off two young Anglo-Australian lads and ran off with them, shouting wildly . . . but already I'm ahead of myself.

For the scene was set when, with their father Simon Howitt, the nine-year-old and 12-year-old lads found themselves just two rows back from the fence in the middle of a wildly enthusiastic Indian crowd who were waving flags, blowing whistles and generally going berserk at any opportunity. Every time an Indian fielder came close to that fence, the Indians went from just berserk to completely insane, as they roared for autographs on caps, shirts, ticket stubs, anything.

The two lads wanted autographs, too, and whenever a fielder obliged and the heaving scrum of Indian supporters surged forward, they shyly hung at the edge of the Indian mass. Suddenly, however, the Indian supporters themselves seemed to notice them and some kind of animated conversation took place in the Hindi language.

The next fielder at fine leg was Suresh Raina, and as he began to move towards the autograph hunters, the two huge Sikhs pounced. Grabbing the caps from the boys' heads, they raced them towards the supporters, shouting and gesticulating. The caps promptly disappeared into the gaping maw of that mass . . . and came back a minute later, with a lovely autograph on each one. Huge smiles all round.

For the troops

I am writing this from Afghanistan, where, believe it or not—I am more than a tad amazed myself—I am part of a travelling troupe of rock bands, etc, entertaining the troops before Chrissie. (My stuff is mostly between sets, telling sports yarns and stuff from some of the war books I've penned.)

One touching thing is that at each Australian base in Kabul, Kandahar and Tarin Kowt, there are myriad sporting posters, paraphernalia and equipment to remind the troops of home. At the initiative of rugby identity Ray Dearlove, they have been gathered from all the main sporting codes, and include AFL flags from all of the clubs as well as balls, many Tennis Australia posters, as well as posters from eight of the 16 NRL clubs, the Waratahs, Cricket Australia, and posters and Socceroo shirts from Football Federation Australia. The Australian Rugby Union was particularly generous in donating posters, balls as well as 500 scarves and 500 caps!

Not one sporting organisation approached declined. Bravo to all, and particularly to Matt Carroll of the ARU and Ben Buckley, formerly of the FFA, who went above and beyond the call of duty.

Miss is a hit

With so many applicants wanting to join Maitland's Blacks team that had won the 2011 Newcastle and Hunter under-11 rugby union premiership, the club decided to enter two teams this year, dividing them evenly by size, skill and speed into the Maitland Blacks and Maitland Whites. In last Saturday's fourth round, the week of State of Origin, the two teams went up against each other on the Maitland Blacks' home field, mate against mate, pate against pate. And what was their fate, and how did they rate?

The lads were hyped and ready to go, evenly matched and went hard from the outset. With a minute remaining, the Whites are leading 17-12, but now the Blacks score in the corner! Can the Blacks convert for a win? He lines it up, he kicks, the ball sails forward, going straight over the black dot.

And then it happens. With every parent from both teams concentrating, the ball starts to shift to the right. Concentrate harder! More to the right! HARDER! And sure enough, the ball hits the right upright, but does not go through.

A wonderful 17–all draw is the result, as both teams and parents congratulate each other.

Fine gesture

A nice scene on the shores of Lake Macquarie last week, as students, parents and coaches of the rowing team of Newcastle Grammar School gathered at Booragul for the annual naming of the boats and launch of the 2012–13 rowing season. Historically, such boats are named after achievers of, or benefactors to, the school's rowing fraternity. But not this time.

This time, while delighting in the gentle sun on their faces and pleasant breeze coming off the water, and contemplating the wonderful, hard rowing to come, their thoughts turned to the 2500 Australians with deteriorating health unable to experience such pleasures because of the failure of one or other of their vital organs. Chained to dialysis machines or an oxygen tank, they are many waiting their turn for all too few organs that become available for transplant.

Thus in an act of social responsibility, the women's quad boat was named 'Donate Life'—encouraging everyone who sees it and hears of it to commit to donating their organs in the event of their death. Bravo.

Swell performance

On a Sunday morning in October, they held the Bondi to Watsons Bay 10 kilometre swim in huge swells, choppy backwash and difficult currents. About 40 solo swimmers and 20 teams competed in the gruelling conditions, which took most swimmers about an hour longer than predicted. The winner, Ryan Huckle, came in on the noggin of three hours, 17 minutes. In another commendable performance, Phil Kearns clocked off at just over four hours, eight minutes.

Most inspiring of the lot, though, was one bloke who made his way to the finish at Vaucluse Yacht Club well over five hours after setting off from Bondi. He touched the boat ramp to the biggest applause of the day. The applause was not simply for the swimmer's triumph over exhaustion, but also because James Pittar is blind. He had been led by a paddler in a kayak who used a whistle to give directions.

Socc it to 'em

You have to imagine the scene. Last Saturday, the undefeated Waverley College under-11E rugby team was meant to play its Knox counterpart. But, as Knox does not have an E side, arrangements were made to host the St Pats 11E rugby team as a replacement. As the boys were warming up at Queens Park, however, it became apparent that the St Pat's rugby team was nowhere to be seen—in view instead was the St Pat's 11E soccer team, sent by mistake.

The teams agreed to play a soccer match and, after trailing 2–0 early, the Waverley boys showed their fighting spirit and turned it around for a 3–2 win and continue their undefeated season with one game remaining—hopefully of rugby.

Hunger fame

Reader Phil Jacombs was walking along the beach with a friend, enjoying a packet of Tim Tams. A white-haired elderly gent coming the other way nodded in greeting and remarked that he loved Tim Tams too:

'So we shared our pack with him and started chatting about life at the beach. He was telling stories of his lifelong love of surfing and I remarked: "Gee, you might have known Snowy McAlister." He replied: "I AM Snowy McAlister!" I was so awestruck at having met an absolute, 22-carat gold surfing legend I couldn't speak any more. My friend had to say goodbye on my behalf. I'll NEVER forget that moment.'

Ineffable coach takes the P

The coach of the Trinity First XV, Ben Morrisey, was giving a spirited address to his adoring team during pre-season training:

'Boys, the key to any game of rugby is just one word. You know what that one word is? It starts with an "F".'

No response from the team, who look at each other blankly.

'*Phases*. Phases of play is the key to any game of rugby.'

Winger (of course): 'That starts with a "P", coach.'

We're told Morrisey was probably joking.

No hiding . . .

Good on the mighty *Blacktown Advocate* for its coverage of one of the more inspiring sports stories of the week. For you see, last weekend the Blacktown Workers rugby league team played the Windsor Wolves, and it did not go well. As a matter of fact, the Blacktown boys were dusted, 74–4.

Nonetheless, Blacktown's coach, the fabulously named Buck Rogers, did not need to be told to buck up. As the paper reported, 'He remains optimistic his team can turn the corner this season.' Exactly! THAT, my friends, is the sort of spirit THIS country was built on! But back to the *Advocate*:

'Following the 74–4 drubbing, Rogers will focus on DEFENCE at training this week in preparation for their clash with The Entrance Tigers on Saturday.' Sounds like a plan. And a last word from coach Rogers: 'We need to work on defence—we're leaking too many points.' Good on him. And the team.

Tour de force

The Tour de Grozzi was started a couple of years ago by Tim Grossman, when his then girlfriend and now wife Di Meagher was undergoing chemo treatment for Hodgkin's lymphoma. All on his ownsome, he set up the bike in pole position in his lounge before the SBS coverage and started to feel he was riding in the 'peloton'. (We bike nutters love that kind of talk!) After sending updates to friends and family, the thing soon turned into the Tour de Grozzi, and Di, once returned from hospital, became the tour manager.

Last year, the peloton grew to five, with four of his tubby mates joining. They set themselves the challenge of clocking up 1000 kilometres over the 23-night duration of the Tour de France, and got their family and friends to sponsor them in achieving this goal with all money raised going to the Leukaemia Foundation. Wives and girlfriends (aka tour managers) reluctantly provided supplies and hydration during many long nights, and last year their goal of $5000 was smashed, with more than $10,000 raised.

Clone this guy

I am reliably informed that, at a recent rugby function where he was a guest speaker, Wallaby Lachie Turner was asked by a member of the Woy Woy under-13s if he could find time to come and watch them play. Turner replied by saying that if they made the grand final he would run the water for them, and kept his word.

When the Woy Woy lads ran out on to Bluetongue Stadium in Gosford, he was there, wearing the Woy Woy strip. He had already helped them prepare, given them a talk and cut the team sheet from the program, which he attached inside his forearm with sticky tape so he knew every boy's first name when he ran on to the field.

The team registered a narrow win and afterwards he had his photo taken with the whole team, before having individual shots taken with every player (and most of the mums).

Fitting sign language

In one of those back lanes in the higgledy-piggedly part of Newtown are a series of rear entrances. Written on one of them, is a sign that reads 'No parking, F—Off!' Five gates down, another reads 'It would be really cool if you didn't park here'.

I am reliably informed by one of their neighbours, who knows both authors of these communications, that they are exactly as you would expect of the people who penned them.

True sports

For more than a year, Yvonne Wallbank, a mother/volunteer with Mosman Swans Junior Australian Football Club, worked to bring an Indigenous team to Sydney to play a game of football against the Mosman Swans' under-11s. Last weekend, she delivered.

Courtesy of donations from Mosman Swans' parents, the Lake Cargelligo Tigers bussed the 550 kilometres from far west NSW on Friday, meeting their new friends from the Mosman Swans at Taronga Zoo, which generously hosted the 30 boys for an overnight 'Zoosnooze', accompanied by Henry Playfair from the Sydney Swans. The lads were then driven to the SCG where the AFL had arranged for the two teams to play the curtain-raiser to the Sydney Swans versus Essendon match, with Mosman and Lake Cargelligo lads mixed into two composite teams before they all formed an honour guard as the Swans ran out.

On Sunday morning, the Lake Cargelligo Tigers and Mosman Swans enjoyed a football clinic with Michael O'Loughlin and Adam Goodes, who volunteered a rare morning off to be there. After an exchange of club caps and shirts, the Lake Cargelligo Tigers boarded the bus for their long trip home. As they departed, the Mosman Swans lined the footpath, waving and raucously cheering them off. Gotta love this country—and the people and sports organisations that make this kind of thing happen.

K's choice

Let's just say that the women of the St Pauls A2 netball team from Winston Hills are predominantly ... 'mature-aged', boasting lots of mothers whose children are twice as tall as the prams they left long ago. No matter. Playing in the Baulkham Hills Shire Netball Association against frequently much younger opponents, this year the close-knit team gave at least as good as they got, and just that little bit more to make the semis.

Alas, in the run-up to that first semi, the team received the news that their 'little general', Kylie Mulcare, had been diagnosed with breast cancer, with her mastectomy scheduled for the following Tuesday. In recognition of her battle to come, for that semi the rest of the team painted a large pink 'K' on their arms, and with Kylie herself leading the way, Winston Hills indeed had a great win.

Last Saturday, without Kylie, it was always going to be harder, but of course they still turned up with their pink Ks proudly displayed. But hang on, what is this? Their opposition in the final, Castle Hills Sports Netball team, were also wearing the pink Ks, as a gesture of sisterly solidarity—something immediately conveyed to Kylie recovering in hospital, which lifted her spirits further.

Fitting result

After a shellacking by St Augustine's the week before, last Saturday the St Andrew's 1st XV had their last game of the season against St Pats Strathfield—a particularly significant day, as it has turned into their annual fundraising game in memory of Kundayi Chiundiza, who passed away after a rugby game for the school two years ago, with the funds going to a school being built in his honour in Zimbabwe.

Played at St Andrews Oval, Sydney Uni, in front of a large crowd of supporters, the St Andrews lads were underdogs from the start but, with the help of a will to win nearly as strong as the wind at their backs, managed to make it to a 5–all score at half-time, and even to 10–all with 20 minutes to go. From this point St Pats spent so much time in the 22 of St Andrew's you'd swear they were paying rent. But tackling themselves red-raw, the locals still held them out until, finally, with three minutes left, St Pats scored in the corner for a commanding 15-10 lead over their exhausted opponents.

Just one last chance now. Retrieving the ball in—where else?—their own 22, and with nothing left on the clock, St Andrew's ruck and maul like men possessed, let it out to the backs, and then ruck and maul some more, as the crowd rises to their feet. Could they? Will they?

Fifty metres out. Forty metres. They're in St Pat's 22. The St Andrews No.8 Filia Talanoa has it, and he is on the charge.

Ramming speed. He breaks the first line, breaks the second line, and sets sail for the promised land until five desperate St Pats cover defenders get to him 10 metres out.

However, as Filia goes down he just manages to flick out a Benji Marshall-esque pass to the hooker, Stu Takau, who hauls it in and heads for the line, even as the remaining defenders race to jump on him. Four metres . . . three . . . two . . . he dives just inside the corner post and . . . try, try, TRY in the corner, try for your life, I'll tell a man it is! It's 15–15 with the kick to come, not that anyone has high hopes of that, so strong and contrary is the wind. In fact, so strong that three times after the kicker sets it up, the wind knocks the ball over. Or maybe it is the gusting squalls of rain.

Still, all the kicker, Zayde Alvarado, can do is try. And no matter that he has already missed two much easier kicks. He lines it up, moves in and connects. The ball takes off like a sick black duck—low, wobbling, weaving, dipping and diving, trying for high altitude but failing miserably. Instead it keeps wobbling near to the ground, heading for the only other thing there that looks like mother duck—the black dot on the cross-bar. As the crowd alternately roars and holds its breath, the ball hits that black dot and bounces up! Up! Up! Up! And . . . over! Goal. A 17–15 victory to St Andrew's, with the St Pats lads being the first to congratulate them.

And that, my friends, is rugby.

Greenwich Village

Since 1988, every four years up Greenwich way they hold what are called the Greenwich Village Games, contested between the Sharpies (who live above River Road) and the Blunts (who live below River Road). Over three days in 20 events, this year's contest was mostly at Bob Campbell Oval with age groups going from the under-7s, to the over-60s, and a non-competitive event for children aged 2 to 6 called the Micro Games.

More than 1000 people participated, with 1500 attending the revue on the Saturday evening. Who won? Who cares?

Howzat!

For the last of the ODI finals games an excited cricket fan took his even more excited 13-year-old son to the big match, using a couple of members tickets given to him by a friend. And yet, as they arrive at the gates—the crowds! the colour! the whiff of history in the air!—there is a problem.

The man and his son are told that while one of the passes gives them access, the other does not. They do not have the money to buy their way to somewhere else on the ground. Deflated, defeated, devastated, the man and his crushed and crying son know there is nothing they can do but trudge back to the car park.

Suddenly, a tap on the shoulder. The father looks around. It is a middle-aged bloke, with a curious expression on his face, proffering him two extremely good tickets, each one marked as being worth $120. He does not want the father to speak. He simply says 'Mate, just make your son happy. That's all.'

Comeback kings

It's like this. Three weeks ago, the Easts Hounds under-12s Aussie rules team played the noted table-toppers Drummoyne Power under-12s, only to be smashed by 100 points. Still they made the finals and, after winning their next match, made it through to last week's grand final, up against the Power lads one more time, on their home ground of beautiful Drummoyne Oval.

Hang on, though, did someone say they'd seen this horror movie before? Perhaps, because after just 10 minutes Easts were down 24-0, in a game in which they'd been lucky to get to 0.

But wait! Doctor, come quickly, I think we have a pulse! For suddenly Easts start to get it together a little, make a few kicks and put together some goals. Their inspirational young captain, Patrick Green, rallies his men and they start to compete. Yes, they're still behind at half-time, but then the former Swan Jason Ball gives them an oration. In urgent, compelling tones, Ball urges them to play for each other, to have guts, believe in themselves and commit to the ball, boys! RAH!

They do just that, and start to haul the Drummoyne lads in, and then pass them! And now they've worked out how to do it, they go on with it. They believe! They COMMIT! And kick! And mark! Gooooooooal! Final score: Easts 69, Drummoyne 45— with the Drummoyne lads being the first to congratulate their opponents on the amazing turnaround.

Golden moment

The scene: the Sydney-wide athletic games for children with autism, held last Saturday afternoon at the Olympic Hockey Centre. The event: the 50 metres dash for seven-year-old boys. The competitor: Joshua Whitcher, who seemed to be not so interested in racing in the event.

Then, in a brilliant display of mentoring, his coach, Alison, who also happens to be his mother, arrived on the scene carrying Joshua's security blanket and his favourite toy, Sylvester the Cat. The coach took up a position in lane 0. The gun went. The coach, the blanket and Sylvester went. And then Joshua went.

At breakneck speed they crossed the finishing line together. The result: Joshua Gold, the coach Gold, Sylvester Gold, the blanket Gold. Gold, gold, gold, gold for Australia, *The Guinness Book of Records* is investigating what is believed to be the first quadruple dead heat in the history of athletics.

Star turn for family

So there reader Matthew Morrison was. Just having a casual bike ride with his two sons, aged 9 and 7, when up ahead on the path he notices Ian Thorpe. In the same instant the Olympian notices them, steps aside, smiles and lets the eldest son through with an encouraging wave and smile. As the lad passes, he and Thorpe exchange a high five, and finally Thorpe allows the youngest son to pass, with lots of cheering and backslapping as he passes.

As Matthew writes, 'It's not often that your kids are cheered on by one of Australia's greatest ever sportsmen!'

True winner

Australia's toughest race, the Six Foot Track Marathon—from the Explorers Tree at Katoomba to the Jenolan Caves 43 kilometres away, and last one there is a pussy—was held last weekend. The last section is the steep footpath that winds its way down from the top of the hill to Jenolan Caves House at the bottom. Long after the winner had breasted the tape, other runners noted a man running down it with his two delighted young lads for the last 500 metres. Crossing the line, his joy was explosive and people smiled happily at his whooping, without knowing the full story.

You see, because the race is so gruelling, there is a cut-off time of seven hours to complete it, and, if you are behind the pace for that, then there are 'sweepers' whose job it is to pull you out of the race. And, 15 kilometres before the end, this fellow had been one so caught. But, very upset, he had argued vociferously with the sweepers, saying he couldn't quit. In fact, he said, 'I shouldn't be here at all—I should be dead'.

Five years earlier, he had been diagnosed with leukaemia, and had only just managed to survive. And now his 10- and 12-year-old sons were waiting for him at the finish line, and he didn't want to disappoint them. But, alas, given his position, the sweepers didn't have any other option and so took his timing tag from him, and left him in the care of the NSW Rural Fire Service volunteers to get him to the finish line in their vehicle, while they ran off ahead.

But then something happened to him. Maybe anger, maybe fear of letting his boys down, or maybe just a second wind. Whatever it was, he was able to start moving again, fast enough that he soon caught up to the sweepers! They returned his timing chip and told him they didn't want to see him again. No worries. With that warning, and with a second chance—at life and in this race—he ran off towards the finish like a scalded hare, met his waiting sons 500 metres out, and had the joy of crossing the finish line with them.

Oi, mate!

In a pub, a fortnight ago, during the Bulldogs vs Manly semi, an old drunk bloke started yelling aggressively at the screen for the Bulldogs to 'go back to Muslim Land' etc etc. He kept going with the same garbage, supported by some laughing dickheads who found it funny, while the rest of the pub turned quiet. Something had to give.

At last it did. One of the younger patrons in a big deep voice called out, 'Oi, mate! Not cool.' The drunk shut up, as did the dickheads, and peace thereafter reigned in the pub, with no more piles of bile. Good on you, mate.

Hospitality multiskilling

Strange days indeed, most peculiar, mama ... A reader was in a major hotel near the airport last week for a conference and searched the foyer for details of the location of the meeting room. Nothing. He went to the young woman at the reception desk and made a polite enquiry as to whether perhaps she might ... I am sorry sir, she interrupted, you will need to speak to the concierge for that information. Oh.

As the concierge desk, about five metres to his left, was unattended, our hero wasn't quite sure what to do but decided to stand in front of it and wait. Bingo! The instant he arrived, the same young woman who had been behind the reception desk appeared. Without a hint of embarrassment, she inquired as to his needs and immediately proceeded to direct him upstairs to the appointed room.

An Olympic feat

'All bound for Morningtown' ... Exactly. And so there April Dixon is on Thursday morning, on her way to work in North Sydney on the train, holding on to the strap when it snaps, and she, in her own words, 'came a gutzer'. And she is hurt, too, badly injuring her knee.

Agonisingly limping her way through North Sydney station during rush hour, the wonderful thing is the many offers of help she receives from complete strangers of all ages, genders, colours and creeds. And she does indeed proceed a little way, leaning on many friendly shoulders. 'It was amazing,' she reports. 'And did a woman's heart good.'

Despite their kindness though, she knows what she needs. As someone who can see the age of 60 just up ahead—with just a few more kilos than she has years—she needs someone of Olympian strength to physically carry her to work at the Australian Children's Music Foundation, a kilometre away up escalators, down stairs, across roads and over ramps.

And there he is now! For here comes her 58-year-old colleague, Peter Hadfield, who represented Australia with distinction as a decathlete at the 1980 and 1984 Olympics. With little ado, Hadfield simply gathers her up in his arms and carries her all the way up the mighty Mount Street, and all the way to work. Faster. Higher. Stronger.

Good man walking

Who says sport and sportsmanship are dead?

In an under-11 junior representative cricket match at Ourimbah last Saturday, between North Shore and Central Coast, the North Shore batsman Callum Snow appeared to be caught behind. And yet the umpire gave the batsman 'not out'. Regardless, Callum—in a manner that would have done Adam Gilchrist proud—put his bat under his arm, removed his gloves and headed back to the pavilion. As the crowd applauded the wonderful display of sportsmanship, the Central Coast team ran to the batsman and roundly clapped him on the back.

The nicest thing? When I mentioned the episode to Gilchrist himself, after jocularly hoping that Callum got less grief from his teammates than he did when he so famously walked, he was very keen to call the lad to congratulate him, and promptly did so. At one point in their conversation, when Gilly asked the young fellow what made him walk, he replied, 'I thought it was the right thing to do, was in the spirit of the game, and . . . I'd had a pretty good bat by that stage!'

Bravo, Callum. Bravo, Adam. Gotta love cricket, when it is played like this.

Prophecy

Six years ago, young Nick Blacklock, then 15 years old, attended the Western Zone grand finals, where Wallaby hooker Tatafu Polota-Nau was presenting the trophies. Having been a fan for a couple of years, Nick asked him for a photo.

Tatafu agreed, but then, looking the strongly built player over and realising he was a young man of ambition, he said, 'We could take a photo now, but why don't we wait until we are playing together and take a photo then?'

Nick agreed and left, more inspired to work hard on his rugby. On Saturday, when Parramatta takes on Randwick at Coogee, N. Blacklock is the loose-head prop, T. Polota-Nau is the hooker. I am sure there will be more than a few photos taken.

Comedian in training

The Auditor-General who came out with the report last week that there are problems not only with our trains, but with the way CityRail communicates those problems to the public is onto something! But at least one of them has a sense of humour about it. One of my friends was on the platform at Sutherland station last Friday afternoon and heard the following announcement croaking through the speakers.

'The 4.30 train to Dapto has been cancelled, [audible groan from those on the platform] ... for today only ... For today, anyway. The train to Central, due on platform one at 4.20, is approximately 10 minutes late ... [more groans]. The train to Cronulla, due on platform three at 4.25, is approximately 20 minutes late ... [resigned sighs]. The train to Waterfall due on platform four at 4.30 is ... on time! [The travellers look at each other, stunned.] Hold on, I'll just check that ... Yes, that's right, the 4.30 train to Waterfall is on time.' (Audible laughter from the long-suffering travelling public.)

That's the spirit

Last Saturday the King's School 4th XI played Sydney High's 4th XI in the GPS Cricket, only for the Sydney High team to be dismissed for zero runs off just 19 balls, with King's bowler Brad Thomas taking 6-0 (including a double hat-trick). With the first run in reply from King's—from a dropped sitter off the first ball of the innings—King's won the game.

Alas, it was far from satisfying. With many of the Sydney High lads having grown up in Asian countries and households where cricket has not been the game of choice, it had been far from a fair contest. But wait. Why stop so soon? One of the King's players, Uday Soni, suggests that rather than all the players going home after such a brief day's cricket, they play a game of Twenty20 cricket in mixed teams. And so they do.

The players split themselves into two teams, each with half King's and half High players and go on to play a game amid great banter, as the usual school loyalties dissipated, replaced by loyalty to the game itself and their new friends. It included a fair deal of friendly instruction on some of the finer points of the game by the King's boys to the High lads—given with compassion and humility, and all taken by them in great spirit.

Well done to King's school captain Jack McCalman and 4th XI captain Hugh Morgan who drove the whole thing. One of the Sydney High players said afterwards that despite being bowled out for a duck, it was the most enjoyable game he had played in six years.

Silence was golden

Last Friday, Col Beszant and 1199 other walkers—divided into 300 teams of four members each—left Hunters Hill High School at 10am bound for Brooklyn on the Hawkesbury in a 100 kilometre endurance race along the Great North Walk, in an event called the Oxfam Trailwalker to raise money for Oxfam Community Aid Abroad.

Deep inside Lane Cove National Park, walking along a track more like Kokoda than the leafy North Shore, the message went up and down the walkers that at 11am all conversation would cease in memory of the last Gallipoli veteran to fall, Alec Campbell.

At 11am, sharp, on a pre-arranged signal all talking stopped and for a minute all that could be heard was the sound of feet along the muddy trail and the falling rain. One minute later a lone voice began reciting . . . 'They shall grow not old, as we that are left grow old: Age shall not weary them, nor the years condemn. At the going down of the sun and in the morning, We will remember them . . .' When done, all the walkers responded with a heart-felt chorus of 'Lest We Forget'.

Incidentally, the winning team on the event, the Royal Gurkha Rifles, smashed the race record and completed the event in 12 hours and 41 minutes! Col's team took 28hr 34min. The rules were you had to finish in under 48 hours, and 800 wounded individuals finally did. They were helped along the way by masses of volunteers offering cheerful words of encouragement.

Young talent time

At the Sydney Football Stadium last Saturday night as the Tahs played the Stormers, a female reader went to a mobile coffee cart and gave her very detailed order to the very young attendant, and was very impressed when the lad both filled out the order correctly and gave her correct change out of $50. His father said that Daniel, aged six, had been helping him in that job since he was three years old.

Bad dog takes the fall

I am promised that the following dinkum happened, on the Wollongong–Southern line just before Chrissie. While waiting for the late arrival of a passenger train, a blind passenger fell from the platform onto the track. Some quick action from fellow commuters allowed him to scramble back onto the platform without too much damage being done.

The station master was obliged to fill in an incident report which he duly did, though he paused when it came to indicating why the incident occurred. After some thought he simply wrote: 'Bad dog'.

Gunner get a goal

Earlier this year, a bloke by the name of Essa Khan, a refugee from Afghanistan via Pakistan, was walking past a gloomy park when, in the semi-darkness, he spies a bunch of blokes kicking a soccer ball around.

One thing leads to another. They prove to be a collection of refugees and asylum seekers, most of them on bridging visas, unable to work, and living on $32 a day . . . don't keep the change. And there are many others just like them, living all around, many having come from Villawood Detention Centre—drawn from as far afield as Afghanistan, Iraq, Iran, Turkey and Tajikistan.

Khan gets busy and finds his way to the Newington Gunners Soccer Club—Newington being that suburb more or less created from the former Sydney Olympic village. With the support of not-for-profit organisation Settlement Services International, a sponsor called Synapse Medical Services and the kindness of strangers, the team is put together, boots and uniforms bought, transport arranged and training facilities secured. They enter into the Granville comp and . . .

And there is a problem at first. See, for most of them, it is their first time actually playing on a field, with lines marked out, a referee, a formal opposition and a crowd. Through interpreters, it has to be explained to them that, while the skills they have learnt playing soccer on the street and in the alleys are fabulous, those skills now have to fit within a framework of rules. Bit by bit, they start to get it. They start to win!

The other teams in the Granville comp welcome them, respect them, and engage with them after matches. Last Saturday they made the final against the Granville Waratahs, at Guildford Park. And it's going to be tough. The Granville men are a tall, tough, physical team, and they have come to play!

A goal midway through the first half puts Granville in front, and the Gunners go into half-time 1–0 down. But are they gunna lie down? Are they, hell! Midway through the second half, Gunners' centre forward Mohammad Mohsin nails a beauty to equalise, 1–1!

Hey ... can you see it coming? Good, because so can the Granville defence.

With seconds left on the clock, Gunner forward Hussain Qalandari jinks left with the ball and then jinks right, as the Granville defenders scramble frantically. But Qalandari's through! Just two Waratahs' defenders and the goalie to go. As they close, however, Qalandri pops a perfect ball to his left and teammate Sajad Hossaini strikes it! Gooaaaaaal! GOOOOOAL! A goal for your life!

The final whistle blows, the Gunners weep for joy and are congratulated by the men of Granville who, despite their disappointment, can't help but feel happy for them. In drinks afterwards, the gracious Granville captain even says that the Gunners deserved to win because they had been the best team all season, on and off the field. RAH!

Meet market

No names, no pack drill. But we're talking about a well-known butcher on the lower north shore, and the scene is set last Tuesday afternoon.

A reader, Mike Cahill, goes in, to find two blokes behind the counter in animated and serious conversation while their fellow worker, a sparkling forty-something woman, attends another customer.

Patiently, our man waits, musing on what might be the urgency of the conversation between the two blokey boners.

Finally, the woman approaches: 'Can I help?'

'Yes, 300 grams of ham off the bone, please. I wonder what those two are gossiping about? Maybe spear tackles in rugby league?'

'I don't know what men talk about,' she says.

'I like to talk about my emotions,' our man smiles.

A pause. And then she continues to weigh and wrap up his order, before leaning in and saying, 'Do you know you have the most beautiful blue eyes?'

A pause.

'So do you. And now, I think we'd better slow down . . .'

'Yes. You're right. Normally I insist on a meal first.'

Coffs calling

Back in 1991, Bill and Helen Ball retired and moved to Sapphire Beach, just north of Coffs Harbour on the NSW north coast. While Helen went back to studies at Southern Cross University, Bill became involved with starting the University Cricket Club and the University Rugby Club, the Marlins. Bill and Helen became quasi-parents to some of the young rugby players, particularly, taking them into their home and doing what they could to help in matters far beyond rugby.

As this year marks 40 years of rugby in Coffs, on the June long weekend the whole rugby community is coming together for a big dinner, with Kick Too Farr Jones as guest speaker. Now, although Bill died a few years back and Helen moved to Bargo, on the way to the NSW Southern Highlands, of course she was invited.

'Alas,' she told them, 'while I would love to come, the pennies don't stretch too far since Bill died. I love you all, hope you have a great time, and I will read about your exploits when you post them on Facebook.'

Ah, but the Coffs rugby community would not take no for an answer, and on Monday Helen received a return airline ticket fully paid for her to attend the dinner.

'I'm a 65-year-old old woman,' she writes. 'I don't know what I've done to deserve this, but in true rugby fashion these men— for now they are men, married some of them, fathers some of them, divorced some of them, with businesses of their own, or jobs to go to—have seen fit to give me this honour. I just want you to know, that this is the meaning of comradeship and honour. They may never win an OAM or a Knighthood, but to me they are the most amazing young men, and I am in awe of them and their families.'

No use grizzlin'

Last Saturday morning, the North Sydney Bears under-10 'Grizzlies' soccer team, boasting one female player, were playing West Pymble at the West Pymble Public School ground 1 and, after just 12 minutes, were losing 4–0—although they at least managed to stem the damage for the next 13 minutes until half-time.

Now, as coach Simon handed out the oranges, did he harangue, hiss, or holler at them in any way? He did not. Instead, he simply said 'Let's forget the first half, Grizzlies, and pretend it's nil-all. Let's see if we can go out and score a goal or two and win the second half. I want you to go out there and enjoy yourselves!' And the Grizzlies did just that, scoring seven unanswered goals against exactly the same opposition, for a 4–7 full-time scoreline.

Farmyard blues

Mike Harvey tells me there was this farmer down Goulburn way, see, and one day a Department of Agriculture rep comes to his door. 'I need a list of your employees and how much you pay them,' demands the official, who'd received a report the farmer hadn't been paying them full freight.

'Well,' the farmer replies, 'there are my hired hands. One has been with me four years; the other for three. I pay each $600 a week, plus free room and board. The cook has been here 18 months, and I pay her $500 a month plus free room and board.'

He hesitates then goes on: 'Then there's the half-wit that works here about 18 hours a day. He takes home $10 a week and I buy him a bottle of bourbon every week.'

'That's the guy I want to talk to, the half-wit,' says the official.

'That,' the farmer says, 'would be me.'

Sporting hero

They held the Australian tug of war titles in Ipswich last weekend, with none other than the Maitland team winning seven out of a possible 10 crowns, plus entry to the world titles next year. The star of the show, nevertheless, was 76-year-old Glen Innes farmer Malcolm Kerr.

The Glen Innes team has a proud history but, like many small country teams, has for the past decade struggled for numbers. At last year's titles in Grafton, Mr Kerr led a young new team with honour and announced his retirement from active competition in favour of a coaching role. But as this year's event rolled around, finding himself with a bare squad of just seven teenagers/young men, one short of the required eight, he decided to strap the boots on one last time.

Of all competitors across all teams over two days, he was the only man to pull in all 10 weight divisions, competing at front man, the hardest position on the rope, against such powerhouse clubs as Maitland, Brisbane and Dumaresq. Late on the second day, his notably lightweight squad should have been flagging, but rallied and took out the 680 kilogram mixed title.

Not for nothing was the loudest cheer at the presentation dinner reserved for him and his lads. Mr Kerr took the opportunity to again announce his retirement. Bravo, Sir. Gotta love this country!

True champion, Part 1

Pennant Hills AFL Club is not the Swans. It's a community-based club that defines the grassroots game, and yet, despite its modest facilities, it has a rich tradition of producing elite AFL players, including Sydney Swans co-captains Kieren Jack and Jarrad McVeigh, and St Kilda champion Lenny Hayes. Plus, as if you didn't know, a long list of others, including the first Sydney-produced player for the Swans when they set up in Sydney in the early 1980s—Terry Thripp.

Die-hards, however, note that beyond the champion players, they've probably never boasted a better man than Barnaby Howarth, who played a season for the Swans before being diagnosed with diabetes and was the Pennant Hills captain back in 2005 when, at just 25, he was so viciously bashed by thugs he suffered a stroke and was in a coma; his family was told to come and say their goodbyes as they prepared to turn off the life support. Somehow, despite it all, after four days he opened his eyes and began his long, long journey back with extensive rehabilitation—starting in a wheelchair and learning how to brush his teeth, shave and hold a fork again. And it went for years.

How long? So long that just three weeks ago, after eight years of working at it every day—to walk again, then jog, then sort of run—he finally received the all-clear to play the four remaining games he needed to make 100 games for the club, a goal he had set himself despite his continuing physical limitations. 'Playing fourth division footy at Pennant Hills is exactly that,' he said after the match. 'It's a normal life. It's perfect. I was a footballer before the stroke, and I'm a footballer now.'

Last week, he played game number 99 for Pennant Hills fourth division and on Saturday—at their old home ground, Ern Holmes Oval at Pennant Hills, where they play one nostalgic game each season—he will run out to play game number 100 to coincide with the Past Players' Day, where former players will visit from far and wide to attend.

Barnaby's sister is flying from Britain for the game, his brother from Perth. On Saturday night, he will retire.

True champion, Part 2

Last Saturday the crowd at Ern Holmes Oval broke all records, and they poured onto the field to form a 70 metres long tunnel as Barnaby Howarth ran out for his 100th game. Their numbers included Penno first grade, the reserves that had just played and their opponents Holroyd Parramatta, as well as Penno's opposition for the day—the mighty Manly Warringah side.

True, in his last three matches Barnaby had struggled to contribute too much, as his vision is still badly impaired, but for this occasion he had some new-fangled sports goggles, meaning that at last the ball was more than a red blur. See? In the first minute of the match, as the crowd roars, he soars like days of yore, takes the mark and kicks the first goal of the match from 35 metres, as his joyous teammates erupt like Vesuvius!

Manly rally though, even as Penno plunders, and it is a hard-fought contest, with Barnaby into everything like pepper and salt. Minutes to go now, and the scores are tight. The umpire blows his whistle. Penno has earned a free kick, but the player has been injured in the tackle and can't take it, meaning the ball should go to the nearest Penno player. And yet, as Barnaby is nearby, a Manly player implores the umpire to give the kick to him. The umpire agrees and Barnaby takes the ball.

It is not going to be easy. A natural left-foot kicker, he has had to learn to kick with his right, as the stroke has affected his left side. He runs forward, drops the ball onto his swinging right foot and . . . connects! The ball sails forth, wobbles momentarily like a sick duck, but then gains strength! WAIT . . .? Is it veering to the right? No, it is straightening . . . Through! GOOOOOOOAL! The winning goal.

The umpire blows the whistle, and Barnaby Howarth, footballer, might well have fallen over, if not for the many hands that lift him high on their shoulders and chair him from the field as his parents cry, his jet-lagged sister who has flown from London for the occasion cries, everyone cries.

The perfect end to a perfect day and the right ending for a long journey all the way back from death's door. In the words of Barnaby himself: 'Put a knife in me, I am done!'

Never miss with Sydney girls

The world is now starting to learn what I and all Australian boys understand intuitively from toddlerdom onwards, just as it has been understood from the very days of the Dreamtime. Australian girls are strong. Australian girls can strike like lightning, and frighten like thunder. You never take on Australian girls, for even when you think you have the upper hand ... ah, boys, those Australian girls will get you in the end. And all of the above goes double when Australian girls have something sharp in their hands!

So all the javelin competitors at the World Youth Championships held in Donetsk, Ukraine, learnt last week. For look there. With one throw to go, Mackenzie Little, the young student from Pymble Ladies College, needs to throw a personal best to win, something made all the more difficult by the breeze and the crowd being against her.

But she is an Australian girl! It is in her blood and in her birthright—Australian girls strike like lightning and frighten like thunder! She hurtles forward, pushes her arm waaaay back—oh yes, back even into the Dreamtime itself—swings it forward and releases!

The javelin traces a perfect arc like the Sydney Harbour Bridge, first soaring high into the crisp stadium air, and even as it slowly descends keeps flying, past her previous throws, past the throws of her competitors, past the point of belief ... and comes to ground . . . with a personal best and Australian record of 61.47 metres!

Say it loud, say it proud: Mackenzie Little—World Youth Javelin champion. Congratulations to her. And let the word go forth from this place and this time, out into the world at large— you never mess with Australian girls, particularly when they're holding something sharp.

Sigh. Australian boys could have told the world that for nuffink.

Stirring the possum

Many moons ago, the late television journalist Paul Lyneham said that, despite a career during which he had interviewed prime ministers and presidents, covered wars, famine and flood, the most reaction he had ever received to a story was when he had done a quick burst at the end of *60 Minutes* complaining about the pain of possums in the roof.

As he told the story, he very shortly thereafter felt a tremor, then a rumble, then a full-blown quake as every computer, every fax machine, every phone at Channel Nine burst into life and kept going for the next week as people from all over the country sympathised and unloaded their theories.

Charity comes knocking

The annual appeal to raise money for the Red Cross kicked off last weekend and will run for all of March. And few will be working as hard as 78-year-old Doris Sutton, of Campsie, who has raised more than $100,000 by doorknocking over the past 20 years, collecting morning and evening over two months. She reckons her most memorable experience was knocking on a door once to find a large man of Middle Eastern appearance, and a rather stern and foreboding one at that.

But this was important. Sutton ploughed on, whereupon the man immediately softened, gave her a hefty donation and fare-welled her with, 'May your god go with you'.

Water baby

Back in 1998, George Corones was, to quote Leonard Cohen, 'just a kid with a crazy dream'. Then 80 years old, and retiring from a lifetime as a doctor and lawn bowler, he took up competitive swimming for the first time in 60 years at the Masters Games. He has been competing ever since—including World Championships events in Christchurch, San Francisco, Perth, Gothenburg and Riccione.

Last weekend he was recognised as the new world champion and record holder in the male 95–99 age group; long course; 50m freestyle, smashing the previous record of 55.88 seconds and taking it down to 47.43! Still not done, he then did much the same in the 100m freestyle, taking it from two minutes, 17.59 seconds to obliterate the two-minute barrier and take it all the way down to 1.57.88. Congratulations, Sir, and so say all of us.

Cowan opens with a nice touch

Australian expat Jason Donald took his eight-year-old son along to the first day of the fifth Test at The Oval and was there in time to see the Australians warming up. As the team left the field, of course, there was a scrum of fans trying to get autographs and, as young Alec is not of the pushy-shovey type, of course he got rather pushy-shovey-ed aside and finished up tucked between the fence and a security bloke.

And who is this striding forth now? Why, it is Ed Cowan, who has had something of a tough Ashes campaign, but knows a young Australian far from home when he sees one. Waving to the security guard, Cowan asks him to let the little kid with the Australian cap come on through, onto the field. Now taking off his gloves, Cowan kneels down, signs young Alec's autograph book, and then gives him the gloves and says, 'Mate, we are three-nil down in England, so you deserve these.'

Alec beams, the crowd cheers, the game begins, and Shane Watson scores 176 runs! A great start to the Test.*

*Cowan was dismissed for a duck in the first innings of the First test and for 14 in the second innings. England won the 2013 Ashes series 3-0

All winners in this tie

You all remember how ugly, cold and wet last Saturday morning was. Well, down on a windswept pitch in Engadine, the mighty under-7E soccer team from Sylvania Heights took on St Pat's in a match played in fine spirit, although no quarter was asked for nor given. But wait!

Midway through the second half, the lace on a Sylvania Heights player's shoe came undone. Well, the player from St Pat's who spotted it did the obvious, didn't he? That is, just as his mum always did for him when his shoelace came undone, he knelt down and tied it up, even as the game was stopped for this uniform malfunction.

Much laughter and applause from players and spectators ensued. Gotta love this country, and junior sport played in this spirit.

Samaritans go extra mile

Last Tuesday at 8.15am David Ray was riding to work on his bike and was hit by a car. He went flying over the bonnet, with his backpack. The driver seemed to have only one word of English, but at least that word 'Sorry . . .' immediately made our man feel better.

The first person to reach him was a woman, who advised him that she was a surf lifesaver and he may be going into shock. She took him through all the key questions to determine if that was the case.

The next person to get involved was a lawyer, who started collecting the information of the driver and the witnesses to the accident. One witness then called the ambulance, which arrived promptly.

The ambos were professional, kind and gentle. They released David to the police, who also proved to be professional, empathetic and efficient.

After all that, one of the female witnesses who had stayed around through it all absolutely insisted on putting his mangled bike in her car and driving him home to the waiting arms of his wife.

It was a long way out of her way but she wouldn't take no for an answer. And all of this in peak hour!

Coming to a full stop

A while back a few blokes were in the Wee Waa pub talking about a local farmer who long ago had inherited a very profitable property, had plenty of hired help and had notoriously always done bugger-all himself. Someone mentioned that he'd retired.

At this point a gnarled and grizzled old shearer in the pub couldn't believe it. 'RETIRED!' he roared, thumping down his beer. 'I bet they didn't find any skidmarks where the bastard pulled up!'

Spirit levels playing field

And speaking of good soccer spirit at a junior level—just stop that bandwagon a moment, would you, as I am trying to get on—at much the same time the Sylvania Heights under-7Es were playing St Pat's, the West Ryde Rovers under-6 team was playing their Roselea counterparts. West Ryde were short of reserves and had a special needs player. Roselea began to score goal after goal, but not for long. Noticing the imbalance, Roselea managers and parents took steps to restrict their own team, forbidding several players from crossing halfway, etc, to make more of a match of it. Bravo.

Knockout memories of rugby great

Lawrence Maher has been feeling a certain sense of sanguine nostalgia this week. He remembers that day in 1963 when he was captaining the Stockton under-14s rugby team in the first match of the season against Waratah in the Newcastle competition. Knowing that Waratah, coached by the late and great Cyril Burke, will be red-hot, Maher tells his forwards to watch out for their little roly-poly halfback, as Burke will have probably taught him a few things. (Translation: 'Get him!')

Sure enough, Stockton kicks off and the halfback catches the ball. And, oh look, he is charging straight towards Maher! 'When he was about a metre from me,' Maher recalls, 'at full speed, he put his head down and rammed me in the stomach. When I came to ... I remember thinking the last thing that flashed before my eyes before he steamrolled me was that ... he seemed to have the features of a man ... encased in a child's body ... 5 o'clock shadow and all!'

Several tries by the halfback later, and with the game over, Maher bothered to learn his name, and he would remember it ever afterwards, as he followed his career: John Hipwell, who went on to be one of Australia's three greatest halfbacks, and also Wallabies captain. Hipwell, sadly, died on Monday* after what appeared to be a heart attack. Vale, John.

Ah, but for Lawrence Maher it got more interesting still. The day after his side got the thrashing from Hipwell's team, Maher was back home, licking his wounds, and decided to go to a suburban shopping centre with a mate, when they came across a singing trio performing on a makeshift stage. They were three skinny, toothy, funny-looking brothers singing in squeaky, high-pitched tones. 'Look at those no-talent bums!' Maher said to his mate.

As it turned out, just like Hipwell, the Bee Gees happened to be pretty good, too!

*23 September 2013

Wilga way

Some 53 years ago, the 17-year-old Daphne Ceeney was riding her boyfriend's former racehorse near the family farm at Murrumburrah. Alas, when it took off across the highway and she tried to rein it in, it suddenly reared up and, slipping on the tarmac, fell back on her, breaking her spine. After 10 months in hospital she was sent home, and frankly wanted to die . . . but mercifully decided against it. After finding out about a program at Mt Wilga Rehabilitation Hospital, which used sport as a tool for rehab, she took up the new sports of wheelchair athletics, fencing, archery and table tennis—as well as swimming. Her life changed forever.

As a matter of fact, she was good enough that with her selection in our team of 12 athletes for the Rome Summer Paralympics in 1960 she became our first female Australian Paralympian, and went on to win six medals at those Games, which proved to be 60 per cent of Australia's total—before following that up with 11 gold medals at the 1962 Commonwealth Paraplegic Games in Perth. The only better shot than her was—if Hallmark Greeting Cards can briefly allow me on their turf—Cupid, who fired the shots that truly counted when, through archery, she met and fell in love with Frank Hilton, marrying him in 1967—three years before she became the first paraplegic to give birth to twins.

Until 2000, she was Australia's highest overall medal winner, with 14 medals in five different sports in three Games. Mrs Hilton now lives in Canberra with her husband, Frank, and turned 80 last week. Congratulations to her. As to Mt Wilga Hospital, it is now a private establishment, but two of its new wards have been recently named after staff who were pioneers of the Paralympic movement in Australia—John Grant and Kevin Betts.

Man invites dog

This comes from the Animal Welfare League's August news-letter, as published in the *Hawkesbury Gazette*.

It seems a man wrote a letter to a small hotel in Mudgee, where he planned a stopover on his holiday. He wrote: 'I'd really like to bring my dog with me. He is well groomed, house-trained and well behaved. Would you let me keep him in my room overnight?'

The reply came from the hotel owner: 'I've been operating this hotel for many years. In all that time I've never had a dog steal towels, bedclothes, silverware or pictures off the wall. I've never had to evict a dog in the middle of the night for being drunk and disorderly. And I've never had a dog run out on a hotel bill. Your dog is very welcome and, if he will vouch for you, you're welcome to stay too.'

Pat Mills for PM!

What a story is that of Pat Mills. His father is a Torres Strait Islander, his mother of the Ynunga Nation in South Australia and, raised in Canberra, he began playing basketball with an Indigenous team his parents started, The Shadows, and starred from the first. 'But still so slight and weedy, one would doubt his power to stay . . .'

At only 1.83 metres fully grown, surely he couldn't really make it in the big time? Think again, after a circuitous route he made it all the way to the San Antonio Spurs and last Monday (AEST) in the fifth match of NBA finals against Le Bron James' Miami Heat, it was our man who in the third quarter nailed five from eight three-pointers to help push his team over the top. He was so dominant that ESPN commentators gave American viewers an impressive lesson in Indigenous Australian history, including the triumph of Eddie Mabo launching his action to secure Aboriginal land rights.

At match's end, Mills covered himself in the Torres Strait Island flag, in honour of his father. 'It's Australian history and we are proud of it,' Mills said afterwards, of ESPN's commentary, and the flag, 'to educate people not just in Australia but overseas was the next level. To use pro basketball to help educate people on our culture is something I've always tried to do—so to have it come off like that was special.'

Learning curve

In the wake of the successful staging of the Bingham Cup in Sydney, the world championship for gay rugby clubs—won by the Sydney Convicts once more—there has been some great writing. One of the best was by a Melbourne rugby player Matt Simpson in *The Roar*, headlined 'Why the Bingham Cup is Important for Straight Men'. The theme was how gay rugby clubs have changed perceptions, and how his team—filled with casual homophobes, including himself—had recently played against the gay Melbourne club, the Footscray Chargers, inviting them back to the club for a drink afterwards.

'The Chargers were fun, social, and had a go at the boat race. They stuck around way longer than most teams. The homophobic that I didn't know I had in me lost a bit more grip. The breaking point came a weekend or two later. Instead of getting rid of the homophobia after the game, we had simply gone back to casual mode, but I think we convinced ourselves it was OK by excusing the Chargers from it. A week after the Chargers game, we were back at the pub, having a beer on a Saturday night as usual. One of our players summoned the rest of the leadership group and me to the smoking area. He came out to us. He was gay.

'My heart sank almost as low as my stomach had dropped. Not only from the guilt I had felt, having put him through weeks of torture [with my casual homophobia], but also the amazing bravery to come out to his own tormentors. He was shaking. We were silent. Then someone asked, "You're still playing though, right?'"

Love that. And yes, he was still playing.

Cutting edge

This is one of my favourite yarns, and it's true! See, at Sydney's Royal Easter Show in 2006, a massive woodchopper, who goes by the simple name of Jed, takes all before him, winning every prize and cutting every log in record time. Everyone is stunned, because he's never shown up in any wood-cutting competition before and no one has ever heard of him.

'Where are you from?' one incredulous journalist asks.

'I'm from the Simpson Forest,' says the axeman.

'Don't you mean the Simpson Desert?'

'Well,' the woodchopper responds modestly, 'that's what they call it now.'

Team mourn

As horrifying murders go, this one was off the scale. As widely reported, 11-year-old Luke Batty was at cricket training with his mates in the small Victorian town of Tyabb on Wednesday afternoon* when his mentally ill father arrived and beat him to death with a cricket bat. There are no words . . . But, what a poignant and touching gesture from the Australian cricket team to wear black armbands on Thursday, in his honour.

*12 February 2014

Banjo shows pluck

I have long maintained that the best thing about rugby is its sense of inclusiveness. If you're fat and slow with no ball skills, you can be a front-rower; a tall work-horse and you're in the second row; an egotist who thinks the whole world revolves around you, and you're at five-eighth; a narcissist who has spent your life running away from physical contact, you're a winger. In recent years, the spirit of inclusiveness has grown, with gay rugby, golden oldies rugby, wheelchair rugby and women's rugby making huge strides. And last year, Trytons rugby was launched—as in "Try TONS!" for kids with mental and physical disabilities, or both. It runs on Saturdays in Maroubra from 11am, while on Sunday another group gather to play at Koola Park in Lindfield from 9am.

When their season started again last weekend, the star of last season was the first one to turn up—eleven-year-old Banjo. As ever, before the session, he practised his goal-kicking, his running and his sidestep. Then, when the others turned up, he ran them all, including the coaches, ragged with his enthusiasm. He loves it. (In his spare time Banjo is the assistant coach of the under-8s at Beecroft, the team his younger brother plays in and where he played early junior rugby.)

Finally Banjo did one more thing. Fearing that the Trytons program might not go ahead again this year, on his own initiative he had launched a fundraising drive. He presented the organisers a cheque for $450. When asked what he wanted them to spend the money on, he asked for a banner for the club march-past before the Waratahs game at ANZ on June 28th, 'To let everyone know what we are doing here'.

Bush humour not drying up

Down Cootamundra way last Saturday night, a bunch of rather depressed farmers were sitting around with their wives, talking about the drought, when they happened to notice the name of the beers they were drinking: Extra Dry and Premium Dry. Then, according to one, Lachlan, it hit them like a frosty morning in July.

Why don't Carlton Breweries bring out a beer called F#$%ing Dry. A percentage from every beer sold could go to some sort of charitable organisation in the bush that is suffering from the economic downturn of drought. Works for me!

Keeping the flame burning

Next time you're caught in a traffic jam on the southerly approaches to the Sydney Harbour Bridge, look to your left, to the Barangaroo building site. On the concrete, marking the floor levels, it doesn't just say '63', it says '63 not out'.*

*Phil Hughes died 63 not out on 27 November 2014 after being hit on the neck by a bouncer during a Sheffield Shield match at the Sydney Cricket Ground

Action man

In a trivia comp last Tuesday, one team had a new face—a bloke called Tom—from Brisbane.

At the half-time break, the subject of rugby came up and, by way of practice, one of the team members, Steve Hall, launched into an impromptu question: 'Who am I?' he asked. 'I'm a famous Australian sportsman who decided to throw a wild pass behind my own try line, losing my team a very important Test.'

Quick as a flash, Tom came back with: 'David Campese, Wallabies v Lions, Sydney Test 1989'.

'Very good,' Steve said, perhaps a tad condescendingly, before having a tiny boast: 'I was at that game. In fact, I was only about five metres from where it happened.'

'So was I,' said Tom with a rueful smile. 'Campo threw that pass and then we got dropped.'

It was, of course, the great Wallabies hooker Tom Lawton, now doing very well in business in Brisbane—with Macquarie, or Ord Minnett, or one of those whizz-bang banking crowds, I can never keep track.

Sari with an Aussie fringe on top

It was a great Australian moment, not quite like mother used to make but still very good.

Early in Thursday night's ODI World Cup semi-final, straight after an Indian batsman had been given out, the camera pans to a 20-something Indian woman, dressed in the colours of her nation of birth, but whose outlook now clearly owes something to Australia.

'Ah, bullshit . . .' says she.

Hooley, dooley, what a yarn

No, I don't believe in angels, or an afterlife, but I do like this story, so shoot me.

See, late last year South Australian Peter Hooley was playing with his US College basketball team, Albany Great Danes, only to receive the appalling news that his mother, Sue, was dying with colon cancer. He immediately upped sticks and went home, to be with her in her final weeks until she did indeed pass away, returning to Albany after missing eight games.

And so there he was last Saturday with his team, up against the Stony Brook Seawolves in the Championship game of the America East Tournament. With three seconds to go, Albany is down by two points, meaning an Albany player had to nail the two-point shot of his life to tie it up.

It arcs beautifully, hits the back board and . . . misses. Bloody thing doesn't go in. But wait!

The ball has gone to our bloke, Peter Hooley, who gathers it in and puts the shot up! She arcs like the Sydney Harbour Bridge and descends with the game in the balance . . . Nothing but net! Three-pointer! Albany wins by a point, with 1.6 seconds left on the clock! Cue pandemonium.

'With angels watching over you, you can do anything,' Hooley said afterwards. Yup. Like I said. But still, his Mum would have been proud.

Manly Roos breed 'em tough

The toughest fellow to have worn the jersey of the mighty Manly Roos junior rugby side? I grant you, Michael Hooper is right up there. But Hooper himself concedes that 11-year-old Rory Williams of Seaforth has him covered.

In mid-November last year, Rory was diagnosed with a rare aggressive tumour the size of a football in his abdomen. The prognosis could not have been grimmer, and in desperation his parents agreed to him being put on an untested clinical trial at Sydney Children's Hospital. Through the whole gruelling process he never complained, but just got on with it, and, miraculously, the tumour—though still present—is now the size of a golf ball. Good.

What Rory most wanted to do was get back to the Roos, and he has done so in the 12As, not missing a game since and playing so well he was named in the Manly Marlins representative side. He has also been playing in the Manly Brothers league team, and this week selected in the under-12s development squad for the Manly–Warringah Sea Eagles! And the whole thing, while continuing his daily cancer therapy and with a tumour still in his abdomen.

A strange aroma

One of my readers went into an ultra-trendy coffee shop in Newtown, a magnet for the beautiful people and a place that prides itself on having the best coffee beans in Sydney. She had an 18-month-old baby with her, which was no problem in itself. But, after she had ordered the coffee and was at a table drinking it, the baby decided it was hungry and wanted to be fed immediately.

No problem. The woman had with her the very thing that the baby often had when it was hungry and took it out, in full public view, peeling back its cover as she went about her business. At this point the staff felt they had to step in.

Could the lady please not feed the baby the mandarin she had taken out, as the aroma from the mandarin would affect the coffee beans and they had to be protected at all costs . . .

Devil of a time for TAS

Last Saturday at Riverview, 700 old bastards with an average age of 50 gathered to compete in the GPS Gold Challenge—essentially GPS old boys competing as in days of yore, and gore, in everything from rugby to rowing, indoor cricket, basketball, footy, athletics, tennis, and much more. Six ambulances and the Zambucks were kept busy till well after sundown, and they ran out of ice—not for keeping the drinks cold, but for ice packs on the hundreds of tender hamstrings.

Big winners on the day were the old boys of The Armidale School who won—wait for it—The Rugby Trophy! It was an extremely popular win. In the words of one participant, 'TAS is like your country cousin that most of the family have long forgotten. Then you catch up for a few beers in the corner at your sister's wedding and you realise he is a really great bloke.' At the dinner, the win for TAS was greeted with a partial standing ovation, by as many participants who could still stand.

In response the TAS captain gloried most particularly in their win over the Old Boys of one school in particular. 'Like most of you we were always smashed by Joeys and felt they were at least five years older than us. Today we slaughtered Joeys and realised we were right. They ARE at least five years older!'

Well played, Waratahs

Yesterday, the Waratahs sent out an Instagram post, wishing all those in the parade down Oxford Street, a HAPPY 2015 Mardi Gras. When a punter posted back 'Wow, I have lost all respect for the Tahs after this post', they didn't delete it. Instead they posted back: 'Dear Justin, Instead of deleting this post, we have left it up here with the hope that you can be educated around this topic. It is extremely important for us as a team that represents the entire state, to be inclusive of everyone who watches and supports us . . .'

These proved to be just their opening remarks, but you get the drift! In fact, in the parade tonight the first cab off the rank is a float honouring those who have served the cause of anti-homophobia in sport, and among those present will be Ellyse Perry, Mike Pyke and Nick Smith, Matt Toomua, Greg Matthews, Paul Langmack, Matthew Mitcham and Daniel Kowalski. Ian Thorpe, alas, is in hospital with a shoulder reconstruction.

Tallangatta CC, ... rings. Tell Thommo, there's a bushfire on the way! He's the local rural bushfire captain. We must hurry.

No time to waste. As the over has just finished, the UHF radio cuts out the message. Thommo, of course, wants to leave immediately. But how? He won't miss Australia, or will it? Of course, the whole mob ...

From Digby S. Scorcher's "Don't Trust the Score" 1966